IMC

INTERNATIONAL
MATHEMATICS OLYMPIAD

6

Prasoon Kumar

V&S PUBLISHERS

Published by:

V&S PUBLISHERS

F-2/16, Ansari road, Daryaganj, New Delhi-110002
☎ 23240026, 23240027 • *Fax:* 011-23240028
Email: info@vspublishers.com • *Website:* www.vspublishers.com

Regional Office : Hyderabad
5-1-707/1, Brij Bhawan (Beside Central Bank of India Lane)
Bank Street, Koti, Hyderabad - 500 095
☎ 040-24737290
E-mail: vspublishershyd@gmail.com

Branch Office : Mumbai
Jaywant Industrial Estate, 2nd Floor–222, Tardeo Road
Opposite Sobo Central Mall, Mumbai – 400 034
☎ 022-23510736
E-mail: vspublishersmum@gmail.com

Follow us on:

All books available at **www.vspublishers.com**

© Copyright: *V&S* PUBLISHERS
ISBN 978-93-579405-5-9
1st Edition

Printed at : Param Offseters Okhla New Delhi-110020

PUBLISHER'S NOTE

V&S Publishers, after the grand success of a number of academic and general books, is pleased to bring out a series of *Mathematics Olympiad books* under *The Gen X series – generating Xcellence in generation X* – which has been designed to focus on the problems faced by students. In all books the concepts have been explained clearly through various examples, illustrations and diagrams wherever required. Each book has been developed to meet specific needs of students who aspire to get distinctions in the field of mathematics and want to become Olympiad champs at national and international levels.

To go through Maths Olympiad successfully, students need to do thorough study of topics covered in the *Olympiads syllabus and the topics covered in school syllabus as well*. The Olympiads not only tests the subjective knowledge but Reasoning skills also. So students are required to comprehend the depth of concepts and problems and gain experience through practice. The Olympiads check efficiency of candidates in problem solving. These exams are conducted in different stages at regional, national, and international levels. At each stage of the test, the candidate should be fully prepared to go through the exam. Therefore, this exam requires careful attention towards comprehension of concepts, thorough practice, and application of rules and concepts.

While other books in market focus selectively on questions or theory; V&S Maths Olympiad books are rather comprehensive. Each book has been divided into five sections namely *Mathematics, Logical Reasoning, Achiever's section, Subjective section, and Model Papers*. The theory has been explained through solved examples. To enhance problem solving skills of candidates, *Multiple Choice Questions (MCQs)* with detailed solutions are given at the end of each chapter. Two *Mock Test Papers* have been included to understand the pattern of exam. A CD containing Study Chart for systematic preparation, Tips & Tricks to crack Maths Olympiad, Pattern of exam, and links of Previous Years Papers is accompanied with this book. The books are also useful for various competitive exams such as NTSE, NSTSE, and SLSTSE as well.

We wish you all success in the examination and a very bright future in the field of mathematics.

All the best

CONTENTS

Section 1
MATHEMATICAL REASONING

1 Playing with Numbers

Numbers

We usually write numbers using the Hindu–Arabic system which uses the ten digits 0, 1, 2, 3, 4, 5, 6, 7, 8 and 9.

Types of Numbers

1. **Even numbers:** All multiples of 2 are called even numbers, e.g., 2, 4, 6, 8, 10, ….. are all even numbers.

2. **Odd numbers:** Numbers which are not multiples of 2 are called odd numbers, e.g., 1, 3, 5, 7, 9 ….. are all odd numbers.

3. **Perfect numbers:** If the sum of all the factors of a number is two times the number then the number is called a perfect number, e.g. The factors of 6 are 1, 2, 3, and 6.

4. **Co-prime numbers:** Two numbers having only '1' as a common factor are called co-prime numbers, e.g., 5 and 8 are co-prime numbers.

Divisibility Tests of Numbers

1. **Divisibility by 2:** A number is divisible by 2 if its ones digit is 0, 2, 4, 6, or 8, e.g., 62, 60, 198, 294 …. etc.

2. **Divisibility by 3:** A number is divisible by 3 if the sum of its digit is divisible by 3.

3. **Divisibility by 4:** A number is divisible by 4 if the number formed by the last two digits (i.e. ones and tens) of the number is divisible by 4.

4. **Divisibility by 5:** A number is divisible by 5 if the digits in ones places is a 0 or 5.

5. **Divisibility by 7:** A number is divisible by 7 if we follow certain steps to determine this:

$623 \rightarrow 3 \times 2 = 6$ (Double the digit in one's place).

$62 - 6 = 56$ (Subtract the number formed by rest of the digits).

$\because$ 56 is divisible by 7.

$\therefore$ 623 is divisible by 7.

6. **Divisibility by 9:** A number is divisible by 9 if the sum of its digits is divisible by 9.

Example 1:　1123056 is divisible by

　　　　　(i) 3　　　　(ii) 5　　　　(iii) 7　　　　(iv) 11

Solution:

(i)　　Sum of digits $= 1 + 1 + 2 + 3 + 0 + 5 + 6 = 18$.

　　　$\because$ 18 is divisible by 3.

　　　$\therefore$ 1123056 is divisible by 3.

(ii)　$\because$ The ones place digit is 6

　　　$\therefore$ The given number is not divisible by 5.

(iii)　$112305 - 6 \times 2 = 112305 - 12 = 112293$

　　　$\because$ 112293 is not divisible by 7.

　　　$\therefore$ 1123056 is not divisible by 7.

(iv)

$$\text{Sum of digits at odd places} = 1 + 2 + 0 + 6 = 9$$

1 1 2 3 0 5 6

$$\text{Sum of digits at even places} = 1 + 3 + 5 = 9.$$

∵ Difference = (9 – 9) = 0

∴ This number is divisible by 11.

Example 2: Check the divisibility of 2345 by 7.

Solution: 234 – 5 × 2 = 224.

∵ 224 is divisible by 7.

∴ 2345 is divisible by 7.

Example 3: Check the divisibility of 9198 by 3 and 9.

Solution: 9 + 1 + 9 + 8 = 27.

∴ the number is divisible by 3 as well as 9.

Example 4: Replace * by the smallest digit, so that it is divisible by 11.

64*719.

Solution:

$$\text{Sum of digits on odd places} = 6 + * + 1 = 7 + *$$

6 4 7 1 9

$$\text{Sum of digits on even places} = 4 + 7 + 9 = 20$$

$20 - 7 - * = 11\lambda$, where, λ is an integer.

For, $\lambda = 1$,

$* = 2$.

Multiples and Factors

Multiple

A number which can be expressed as a product of two or more numbers is called the multiple of those numbers. For example 42 is a multiple of 6 as well as 7.

Factor

A factor is the number which divides the given number completely by leaving remainder '0'. For example 28 is divisible by 1, 2, 4, 7 and 28. So these are factors of 28.

Highest Common Factor

The largest common factor of two or more numbers is their Highest Common Factor (HCF). It is also known as Greatest Common Divisor (GCD).

The possible factors of 42 are 1, 2, 3, 6, 7, 14, 42.

The possible factors of 56 are 1, 2, 4, 7, 8, 14, 28, 56.

∴ The highest common factor of 42 and 56 = 14.

There are two methods to find H.C.F. of given numbers:

1. Prime Factorisation Method,
2. Division Method.

Example 5:   Find the H.C.F. of 270 and 729 by prime factorization method.

Solution:

2	270
3	135
3	45
3	15
	5

3	729
3	243
3	81
3	27
3	9
	3

$270 = 2 \times 3 \times 3 \times 3 \times 5$ and
$729 = 3 \times 3 \times 3 \times 3 \times 3 \times 3$
∴ H.C.F. of 270 and 729 = $3 \times 3 \times 3 = 27$.

Example 6:   Find the HCF of 120 and 96 by division method.

Solution:

$$96 \overline{)120} (1$$
$$\underline{96}$$
$$24 \overline{)96} (4$$
$$\underline{96}$$
$$\times\times$$

∴ HCF of 120 and 96 = 24.

HCF of Three or More Numbers

Example 7:   Find the greatest number which divides 13, 133, 37 leaving 1 as a remainder.

Solution:

13	133	37
−1	−1	−1
12	132	36

Hence, the required number is H.C.F. of 12, 132 and 36.
∴ HCF of 12 and 132

$$12 \overline{)132} (11$$
$$\underline{12}$$
$$12$$
$$\underline{12}$$
$$\times\times$$

HCF of 12 and 132 = 12.
Similarly, HCF of 12 and 36 = 12.
∴ HCF of 12, 132, and 36 = 12.
∴ Required number = 12.

Lowest Common Multiple (LCM)

The lowest common multiple of two or more numbers is the smallest number which is multiple of each of the given numbers.

There are two methods to find LCM of given numbers.

  (i)   Prime factorisation method
  (ii) Division method

Example 8: Find the LCM of 4, 16, 20, 24 and 36.

Solution:

2	4, 16, 20, 24, 36
2	2, 8, 10, 12, 18
2	1, 4, 5, 6, 9
3	1, 2, 5, 3, 9
	1, 2, 5, 1, 3

∴ LCM of 4, 16, 20, 24 and 36 = $2 \times 2 \times 2 \times 3 \times 2 \times 5 \times 3 = 1440$.

Example 9: Four bells toll at intervals 5, 10, 15 and 25 seconds. The bells toll together of 6 O'clock. When will they toll together again?

Solution: Time when the bells will toll together = LCM of 5, 10, 15 and 25.

5	5, 10, 15, 25
	1, 2, 3, 5

LCM of 5, 10, 15 and 25 = $5 \times 2 \times 3 \times 5$

$= 150$ seconds.

∴ 150 seconds = 2.5 min.

∴ Bells will again toll 2.5 minutes past 6 o'clock.

Relation between HCF and LCM of Two Numbers

For any two numbers 'x' and 'y',

Product of x and y = HCF of x and y × LCM of x and y.

Example 10: The HCF of two numbers is 4 and their product is 288. Find the LCM of two numbers.

Solution: LCM × HCF = Product of numbers.

$$\therefore LCM = \frac{\text{product of numbers}}{\text{HCF}}$$

$$= \frac{288}{4}$$

$$= 72$$

1. The HCF of two numbers is 16 and their product is 3072. What is the LCM?
   (a) 182   (b) 162
   (c) 192   (d) 196

2. Which of the following numbers is divisible by 3?
   (a) 24357806   (b) 33336433
   (c) 35769812   (d) 83479560

3. Which of the following is a prime number?
   (a) 117   (b) 171
   (c) 179   (d) 169

4. Which of the following is not a twin prime?
   (a) (11, 13)   (b) (17, 19)
   (c) (23, 29)   (d) (41, 43)

5. Find the greatest number which divides 126, 150 and 210 leaving remainder 6 in each case.
   (a) 12   (b) 14
   (c) 16   (d) 22

6. Find the largest number that will divide 76, 113 and 186 leaving remainder 4, 5, 6 respectively.
   (a) 24   (b) 12
   (c) 36   (d) 54

7. Find the smallest number which when divided by 16, 36 & 40 leaves a remainder 7 in each case.
   (a) 627   (b) 727
   (c) 827   (d) 927

8. Which greatest number of 4 digits is exactly divisible by 12, 16, 28 & 36?
   (a) 6072   (b) 8072
   (c) 8972   (d) 9072

9. The HCF of two numbers is 23 and their LCM is 1449. If one of the numbers is 161 what is the other?
   (a) 107   (b) 117
   (c) 167   (d) 207

10. Find the smallest number which when diming by 3 is divisible by 21, 28, 36 and 45?
    (a) 1163   (b) 1263
    (c) 1283   (d) 1293

11. The HCF of two numbers is 145 and their LCM is 2175. If one of the numbers is 725. What is the other number?
    (a) 5   (b) 290
    (c) 115   (d) 435

12. Which of the following is a composite number?
    (a) 23   (b) 29
    (c) 32   (d) 41

13. Which longest tape can be used to measure exactly the length 7m, 3m 85cm and 12m 95 cm?
    (a) 45 cm   (b) 35 cm
    (c) 105 cm   (d) 70 cm

14. The greatest number that will divide 445, 572 & 699 leaving remainder 4, 5, 6 respectively.
    (a) 84   (b) 42
    (c) 49   (d) 63

15. What is the sum of LCM & HCF of 1152 & 1664?
    (a) 14976   (b) 15104
    (c) 15114   (d) 15204

16. The HCF of two numbers is 21 and their LCM is 3003. If one of the numbers is 231. Then what is the other number?
    (a) 273   (b) 263
    (c) 283   (d) 293

17. Find the greatest 3-digit number which is divisible by 8, 10 and 12.
    (a) 840   (b) 480
    (c) 960   (d) 980

18. Which of the following number is not divisible by 9?
    (a) 387459   (b) 904806
    (c) 758934   (d) 879134

19. Find the smallest possible number which on adding 19 becomes exactly divisible by 28, 36 and 45.

(a) 1239   (b) 1241

(c) 1243   (d) 1245

20. Four bells toll at intervals 4, 7, 12 & 84 seconds. The bells toll together at 7 o'clock. How many times will they again toll together in 28 minutes?

(a) 15   (b) 20

(c) 25   (d) 30

21. What is the least 5-digit number which is exactly divisible by 20, 25, 30?

(a) 10100   (b) 10200

(c) 10300   (d) 10400

22. What is the maximum even multiple of 25 between 500 & 700?

(a) 660   (b) 600

(c) 675   (d) 650

23. Which of the following number is divisible by 8?

(a) 162537   (b) 764918

(c) 825908   (d) 694728

24. Which of the following is divisible by 11?

(a) 65483   (b) 72493

(c) 84527   (d) 92056

25. What is sum of first five multiples of 23?

(a) 341   (b) 342

(c) 343   (d) 345

26. Which of the following statement is true?

(a) 1509344 is divisible by 8.

(b) 72493 is divisible by 11.

(c) 8569 is not divisible by 11.

(d) 115 is a multiple of 19.

27. In 467 * 381 replace * by which smallest digit to make it divisible by 3?

(a) 1   (b) 2

(c) 3   (d) 4

28. 1870 is divisible by 22. Which two numbers nearest to 1870 are each divisible by 22?

(a) 1848, 1892   (b) 1893, 1914

(c) 1826, 1914   (d) None of these

29. There are three heaps of rice weighing 120 kg, 144 kg and 204 kg. What is the maximum capacity of a bag so that the rice of each can be packed in exactly number of bags?

(a) 24 kg   (b) 18 kg

(c) 12 kg   (d) 6 kg

30. Four bells ring at intervals of 6, 8, 12 & 20 minutes. They ring simultaneously at 7 a.m. At what time will they ring together?

(a) 8 a.m.   (b) 9 a.m.

(c) 10 a.m.   (d) 9:30 a.m.

Answer Key

1. (c)	2. (d)	3. (c)	4. (c)	5. (a)	6. (c)	7. (b)	8. (d)	9. (d)	10 (b)
11. (d)	12. (c)	13. (b)	14. (d)	15. (b)	16. (a)	17. (c)	18. (d)	19. (b)	20. (b)
21. (a)	22.(d)	23. (d)	24. (a)	25. (d)	26. (a)	27. (a)	28. (a)	29. (c)	30. (b)

1. **(c)** HCF × LCM = product of numbers.

$$\Rightarrow LCM = \frac{\text{Product of numbers}}{HCF}$$

$$= \frac{3072}{16} = 192$$

2. **(d)**

   $2 + 4 + 3 + 5 + 7 + 8 + 0 + 6 = 35$

   $3 + 3 + 3 + 3 + 6 + 4 + 3 + 3 = 28$

   $3 + 5 + 7 + 6 + 9 + 8 + 1 + 2 = 41$

   $8 + 3 + 4 + 7 + 9 + 5 + 6 + 0 = 42$

   Since 42 is divisible by 3 then (d) is divisible by 3.

3. **(c)**

   117, 171 are divisible by 3.

   169 is divisible by 13.

   179 is a prime number.

4. **(c)**

   (23, 29) is not a twin prime.

5. **(a)**

126	150	210
− 6	− 6	− 6
120	144	204

   LCM of 120 and 144 = 12

   LCM of 120 and 204 = 12

   Required number = LCM of 120, 144, 204

   $$= 12$$

6. **(c)**

76	113	186
− 4	− 5	− 6
72	108	180

   HCF of 72 and 108 = 36

   HCF of 108 and 180 = 36

   ∴ required number = 36

7. **(b)**

   LCM of 16, 36 and 40 is

2	16, 36, 40
2	8, 18, 20
2	4, 9, 10
	2, 9, 5

   ∴ LCM = 2 × 2 × 2 × 2 × 9 × 5

   $$= 16 × 45 = 720$$

   ∴ required number = (720 + 7) = 727

8. **(d)**

   The greatest 4 digit number = 9999.

   Here,

2	12, 16, 28, 36
2	6, 8, 14, 18
2	3, 4, 7, 9
	3, 2, 7, 3

   LCM of 12, 16, 28 and 36

   $$= 2 × 2 × 2 × 3 × 2 × 7 × 3$$
   $$= 4 × 9 × 4 × 7$$
   $$= 16 × 9 × 7$$
   $$= 1008$$

   ∵ 9072 is a multiple of 1008.

   ∴ it is the greatest number of 4 digits which is divisible by 12, 16, 28 & 36.

9. **(d)**

   LCM × HCF = one number × second number

   $$\Rightarrow \text{Second number} = \frac{23 \times 1449}{161}$$
   $$= 23 × 9$$
   $$= 207$$

10. (b)

LCM of 21, 28, 36 and 45 is

3	21, 28, 36, 45
2	7, 28, 12, 15
3	7, 14, 6, 15
2	7, 14, 2, 5
7	7, 7, 1, 5
	1, 1, 1, 5

$\therefore$ LCM of 21, 28, 36 and 45

$\quad = 3 \times 2 \times 3 \times 2 \times 7 \times 5$

$\quad = 36 \times 35$

$\quad = 1260$

$\therefore$ Required number = 1260 + 3 = 1263

11. (d)

Required number $= \dfrac{\text{HCF} \times \text{LCM}}{\text{one of the numbers}}$

$\quad = \dfrac{145 \times 2175}{725}$

$\quad = 435$

12. (c)

$\because$ 32 has 1, 2, 4, 8, 16, 32, as its factors.

$\therefore$ 32 is a composite number.

13. (b)

Required length = HCF of 700, 385 and 1295

$\quad\quad\quad\quad\quad = 35\text{cm}$

14. (d)

$$\begin{array}{ccc} 445 & 572 & 699 \\ -4 & -5 & -6 \\ \hline 441 & 567 & 693 \end{array}$$

3	441
3	147
7	49
	7

3	567
3	189
3	63
3	21
	7

3	693
3	231
7	77
	11

HCF of 441, 567 and 693 = $3 \times 3 \times 7$

$\quad\quad\quad\quad\quad\quad\quad\quad\quad = 63$

$\therefore$ Required number $\quad = 63$

15. (b)

HCF of 1152 and 1664

2	1152
2	576
2	288
2	144
2	72
2	36
2	18
3	9
	3

2	1664
2	832
2	416
2	208
2	104
2	52
2	26
	13

$\therefore$ HCF of 1152 and 1664 = 2^7 = 128

and LCM of 1152 and 1664 = 14976

2	1152, 1664
2	526, 832
	263, 416

$\therefore$ LCM + HCF = 14976 + 128 = 15104.

16. (a)

Required number $= \dfrac{21 \times 3003}{231}$

$\quad\quad\quad\quad\quad\quad = 273$

17. (c)

LCM of 8, 10 and 12

2	8, 10, 12
2	4, 5, 6
	2, 5, 3

$\therefore$ LCM of 8, 10, 12 = $2 \times 2 \times 2 \times 5 \times 3$

$\quad\quad\quad\quad\quad\quad\quad\quad = 120$

$\therefore$ Greatest 3-digit number which is divisible by 8, 10 and 12 = $120 \times 8 = 960$

18. (d)

3 + 8 + 7 + 4 + 5 + 9 = 36

9 + 0 + 4 + 8 + 0 + 6 = 27

7 + 5 + 8 + 9 + 3 + 4 = 36

8 + 7 + 9 + 1 + 3 + 4 = 32

$\because$ 32 is not divisible by 9.

$\therefore$ 879134 is not divisible by 9.

19. **(b)**

LCM of 28, 36 and 45

2	28, 36, 45
2	14, 18, 45
3	7, 9, 45
3	7, 3, 15
	7, 1, 5

∴ LCM of 28, 36 and 45

$$= 2 \times 2 \times 3 \times 3 \times 7 \times 5$$
$$= 4 \times 9 \times 35$$
$$= 140 \times 9$$
$$= 1260$$

∴ Required number $= 1260 - 19$
$$= 1241$$

20. **(b)**

LCM of 4, 7, 12 and 84 =

2	4, 7, 12, 84
2	2, 7, 6, 42
3	1, 7, 3, 21
7	1, 7, 1, 7
	1, 1, 1, 1

$$= 2 \times 2 \times 3 \times 7 = 84 \text{ seconds.}$$

∴ The bells will toll together after 84 seconds.

∴ Number of times the bells will toll together in 28 minutes $= \dfrac{28 \times 60}{84} = 20$

21. **(a)**

LCM of 20, 25, 30 is

2	20, 25, 30
5	10, 25, 15
	2, 5, 3

∴ LCM of 20, 25, 30 $= 2 \times 5 \times 2 \times 5 \times 3$
$$= 300$$

∴ least 5-digit number which is exactly divisible by 20, 25, 30 = 10100.

22. **(d)**

Multiples of 25 between 500 and 700 = 525, 550, 575, 600, 625, 650, 675.

∴ Required number = 650

23. **(d)**

694728 is divisible by 2 as well as 4.

∴ 694728 is divisible by 8.

24. **(a)**

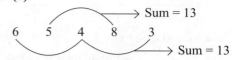

Difference $= 13 - 13 = 0$

∴ 65483 is divisible by 11.

25. **(d)**

Sum of first five multiples of $23 = 23 + 23 \times 2 + 23 \times 3 + 23 \times 4 + 23 \times 5$

$$= 23 (1 + 2 + 3 + 4 + 5)$$
$$= 23 \times 15$$
$$= 345$$

26. **(a)**

1509344 is divisible by 8.

27. **(a)**

467 * 381

The sum of digits of the above number

$$= 4 + 6 + 7 + * + 3 + 8 + 1$$
$$= 10 + 7 + * + 3 + 8 + 1$$
$$= 29 + *$$

If, $* = 1$, then, the sum of digits will become 30.

∴ required number = 1

28. **(a)**

$$1870 + 22 = 1892$$
$$1870 - 22 = 1848$$

29. **(c)**

Required capacity of bag

$$= \text{HCF of } 120, 144 \text{ and } 204$$
$$= 12 \text{ kg}$$

30. **(b)**

Required time = LCM of 6, 8, 12 and 20

2	6, 8, 12, 20
2	3, 4, 6, 10
3	3, 2, 3, 5
	1, 2, 1, 5

$\therefore$ Required time = $2 \times 2 \times 3 \times 2 \times 5$

$\qquad\qquad$ = 120 minutes = 2 hr.

$\therefore$ bells will again ring together at (7 + 2)

$\qquad\qquad\qquad\qquad$ = 9 a.m.

Notation: Writing a number in figures is called notation.

Numeration: Writing a number in words is called numeration.

Numeral: A group of digits, denoting a specific number is called a numeral.

System of Writing Numbers

Hindu–Arabic System

In this system, we use ten symbols, namely 0, 1, 2, 3, 4, 5, 6, 7, 8, 9 called digits or figures, to represent any number.

Example 1:   Write 2623 in expanded form and hence write it in words.

Solution: $2623 = (2 \times 1000) + (6 \times 100) + (2 \times 10) + 3$.

∴ 2623 can be read as 'Two thousand six hundred and twenty three.'

Example 2:   Express 823415 in words.

Solution: 823415 = Eight lakhs twenty three thousand four hundred and fifteen.

Face Value and Place Value of a Digit

Face Value

The face value of a digit remains as it is, what place it may be occupying in the place value chart.

For example: The face value of 3 in 2345 will be 3.

Place Value

The place value of a digit in a numeral depends upon the place it occupies in the place value chart.

For determining the place value of a digit in a number replace all the digits in the number, right to the digit whose place value is to be determined by zero.

Example 3:   What is the place value of 5 in 25342 ?

Solution: Place value of 5 in $25342 = 5 \times 1000 = 5000$

Example 4:   How many 6 digits numbers are there in all?

Solution: The largest 6 – digit number = 999999

The smallest 6 – digit number = 100000

∴ Number of 6 – digit numbers = $(999999 - 100000) + 1$

$= 899999 + 1$

$= 900000$

Example 5:   Write the smallest 5 digit number having

(i) all same digits.

(ii) all different digits.

Solution: The smallest 5 – digit number = 10000

(i) ∴ The smallest 5 – digit number having all same digits = 11111

(ii) The smallest 5 – digit number having all different digits = 10234

Comparison of Numbers

Example 6: Which is greater : 1023468 or 2345689?

Solution: The number of digits in 1023468 = 7

The number of digits in 2345689 = 7

∴ We compare the first digit of the numbers.

∵ 2 > 1

∴ 2345689 > 1023468

Example 7: The cost of a table is ₹ 2265. What will be the price of 223 such tables?

Solution: Cost of 223 tables = ₹ (2265 × 223)

= ₹ 505095

Estimation

Example 8: Estimate the sum (665 + 463) to the

(i) nearest hundred,

(ii) nearest ten,

(iii) nearest thousand

Solution:

(i) Estimation of 665 to nearest hundred = 700

Estimation of 463 to nearest hundred = 500

∴ estimated sum = (700 + 500) = 1200

(ii) Estimation of 665 to nearest ten = 670

Estimation of 463 to nearest ten = 460

∴ estimated sum = 670 + 460 = 1130

(iii) Estimation of 665 to nearest thousand = 1000

Estimation of 463 to nearest thousand = 0

∴ estimated sum = 1000

Example 9: Estimate the product 46 and 59.

Solution: Estimation of 46 to nearest ten = 50

Estimation of 59 to nearest ten = 60

∴ Product (estimated) = 50 × 60

= 3000

Example 10: Estimate the quotient : 276 ÷ 21

Solution: Estimation of 276 to nearest ten = 280

Estimation of 21 to nearest ten = 20

∴ estimated quotient = 280 ÷ 20

= 14

Roman Numerals

We write numbers using the Hindu-Arabic system which uses the ten digits 0, 1, 2, 3, ...9. Numbers can also be written using seven Roman Numerals.

Hindu Arabic numeral   ⟶   Roman numeral

1   ⟶   I

5   ⟶   V

10   ⟶   X

$$50 \rightarrow L$$
$$100 \rightarrow C$$
$$500 \rightarrow D$$
$$1000 \rightarrow M$$

Rules for Writing Roman Numerals

Rule 1. When a roman numeral is placed after another of greater value, the value of the resulting numeral is equal to the sum of the numerals.

Example: XV = 10 + 5 = 15

XII = 10 + 2 = 10

Rule 2. When a roman numeral is placed before another of greater value, the value of the resulting numeral is equal to the difference of the numerals.

Example: IX = 10 – 1 = 9

XC = 100 – 10 = 90

Rule 3. When a roman numeral of smaller value is put between two numerals of greater value, it is subtracted from the number on its right.

Example: XIX = 10 + 10 – 1 = 19

XIV = 10 + 5 – 1 = 14

Rule 4. When certain roman numerals are repeated, the number represented by them is their sum.

Example: XV = 10 + 5 = 15

XII = 10 + 2 = 10

Note 1. There is no roman numeral for zero.

2. Roman numberals do not follow the place value system.

Example 11: Express 215 as roman numeral.

Solution: 215 = 200 + 15 = 100 + 100 + 10 + 5

= C C X V

Example 12: Express CXIV in Hindu – Arabic system.

Solution: CXIV = C + X + IV

= 100 + 10 + 4 = 114

Example 13: Express CM as Hindu – Arabic numeral.

Solution: CM = (1000 – 100) = 900

Example 14: Which of the following roman numerals is (are) meaningless?

(a) XXXX   (b) XVV

(c) XLVI   (d) IC

(e) CCCXL

Solution: (a) ∵ No symbol can be repeated more than 3 times.

∴ XXXX is meaningless.

(b) ∵ V, L and D are never repeated.

∴ XVV is meaningless.

(c) XLVI ⇒ X + L + V + I = 56 – 10 = 46

(d) IC ⇒ I can never subtracted from C. ∴ IC is meaningless.

(e) CCCXL ⇒ This is meaningful.

1. What is the face value of 4 in the numeral 76247709?
   (a) 40000   (b) 4
   (c) 47709   (d) 7824

2. The smallest counting number is
   (a) 1   (b) 10
   (c) 0   (d) None of these

3. What is the value of CLXVI?
   (a) 146   (b) 156
   (c) 166   (d) 176

4. The product of two numbers is 33755631. If one number is 42567, then what is the other number?
   (a) 493   (b) 693
   (c) 793   (d) 893

5. What is the nearest thousand of the sum 21297 + 27867 + 42679 ?
   (a) 91000   (b) 92000
   (c) 89000   (d) 90000

6. What is the round off value of the product 43 and 78 ?
   (a) 2800   (b) 3200
   (c) 3500   (d) 3510

7. What number must be subtracted from 1101010 to get 336414 ?
   (a) 754696   (b) 765496
   (c) 764569   (d) 764596

8. The population of a town in the year 2010 was 14693675. In the following year, the population became 18002403. What is the increase in the population?
   (a) 3308728   (b) 3327827
   (c) 3306728   (d) 3206728

9. In the given numbers which will exactly come in the middle?
   3307, 3279, 3467, 3502, 3379, 3667, 3287
   (a) 3307   (b) 3379
   (c) 3467   (d) 3287

10. For making 16 shirts 44 metres of cloth is needed. How much cloth is required for 4 shirts?
    (a) 10m   (b) 11m
    (c) 12m   (d) 13m

11. A rope of length 20m has been divided into 8 pieces of the same length. What is the length of each piece?
    (a) 1.25m   (b) 2.25m
    (c) 2.50m   (d) 2.75m

12. By how much 5943679 smaller than one crore?
    (a) 4056321   (b) 4146321
    (c) 4066321   (d) 4056221

13. Mr. Sharma saves ₹ 8719 every month. How much money will he save in 12 years?
    (a) ₹ 1255636   (b) ₹ 1255036
    (c) ₹ 1255536   (d) ₹ 1255736

14. A motorcycles costs ₹ 49735. How much will 487 motorcycles cost?
    (a) ₹ 24222945   (b) ₹ 24221945
    (c) ₹ 24210945   (d) ₹ 24220945

15. If 18 flats cost ₹ 68251500. What is the cost of each flat?
    (a) ₹ 3791750   (b) ₹ 3797250
    (c) ₹ 3791250   (d) ₹ 3791500

16. What is the difference between the number 768 and that obtained on reversing its digits?
    (a) 97   (b) 98
    (c) 99   (d) 109

17. What is the sum of the number 387 and the number obtained by reversing the digit of the given number?
    (a) 1160   (b) 1170
    (c) 1070   (d) 1150

18. What is the roman numeral for 92 ?
    (a) XCII   (b) CXII
    (c) LXXXXII   (d) LXIV

19. Which of the following is an invalid number
    (a) XXXX
    (b) XCIX
    (c) XLVI
    (d) CCCXL

20. What is the Hindu – Arabic numeral for CDXLVI ?
    (a) 442
    (b) 446
    (c) 448
    (d) 456

21. What is the difference of place value and face value of 7 in the number 30972 ?
    (a) 63
    (b) 65
    (c) 965
    (d) 963

22. A car covers 570 km in 16 hours. What is the speed of the car?
    (a) 35 km 625 km/h
    (b) 35 km 325 km/h
    (c) 35 km 425 km/h
    (d) 35 km 525 km/h

23. Which of the following is meaningful?
    (a) XXXX
    (b) XVV
    (c) IC
    (d) XCI

24. A factory produces 6097 screws per day. How many screws will it produce in the month of September 2015 ?
    (a) 182941
    (b) 182910
    (c) 189007
    (d) None of these

25. By how much is 7346879 smaller than one crore?
    (a) 2653151
    (b) 2653141
    (c) 2653131
    (d) 2653121

26. The mass of each gas cylinder is 14kg 250-g a what is the total mass of 19 such cylinders?
    (a) 270.25kg
    (b) 272.75kg
    (c) 270.75kg
    (d) None of these

27. The difference between two numbers is 9470587. If the smaller number is 6976583, what is the greater number?
    (a) 16457170
    (b) 16447170
    (c) 16447071
    (d) 16437170

28. Which of the following is correct?
    (a) 29047 > 29153 > 28956
    (b) 28043 > 27654 > 26098
    (c) 30067 > 29804 > 29987
    (d) 40167 > 42157 > 42117

29. A number exceeds 3760924 by 39067. What is that number?
    (a) 3799871
    (b) 3799891
    (c) 3799991
    (d) None of these

30. The cost of a table is ₹ 1479. How much will 479 chairs cost?
    (a) ₹ 706441
    (b) ₹ 708441
    (c) ₹ 707441
    (d) None of these

Answer Key

1. (b)	2. (a)	3. (c)	4. (c)	5. (b)	6. (b)	7. (d)	8. (a)	9. (b)	10 (b)
11. (c)	12. (a)	13. (c)	14. (d)	15. (a)	16. (c)	17. (b)	18. (a)	19. (a)	20. (b)
21. (a)	22.(a)	23. (d)	24. (b)	25. (d)	26. (c)	27. (b)	28. (b)	29. (c)	30. (b)

1. **(b)**

2. **(a)**

3. **(c)**

   CLXVI = 100 + 50 + 10 + 5 + 1 = 166

4. **(c)**

   Other number = $\dfrac{33755631}{42567}$ = 793

5. **(b)**

   21297 + 27867 + 42679

       = 21000 + 28000 + 43000

       = 92000

6. **(b)**

   43 × 78

       = 40 × 80 = 3200

7. **(d)**

   1101010 − 336414

       = 764596

8. **(a)**

   Increase in population = 18002403 − 14693675

                        = 3308728

9. **(b)**

   Numbers in ascending order are 3279, 3287, 3307, (3379), 3467, 3502, 3667.

10. **(b)**

    Cloth required for 4 shirts = $\dfrac{44}{16} \times 4$ = 11m

11. **(c)**

    Length of each piece = $\dfrac{20}{8}$ = 2.5m

12. **(a)**

    10000000 − 5943679 = 4056321

13. **(c)**

    Required amount = 8719 × 12 × 12

                   = ₹ 1255536

14. **(d)**

    Required amount = 49735 × 487

                   = ₹ 24220945

15. **(a)**

    Cost of each flat = $\dfrac{68251500}{18}$ = ₹ 3791750

16. **(c)**

    Required difference = 867 − 768 = 99

17. **(b)**

    Required value = 387 + 783 = 1170

18. **(a)**

    XCII = (100 − 10) + 1 + 1 = 92

19. **(a)** XXXX is meaningless.

20. **(b)**

    CDXLVI = (500 − 100) + (50 − 10) + 5 + 1

             = 400 + 40 + 6

             = 446

21. **(a)**

    Required difference = 70 − 7 = 63

22. **(a)**

    Speed of the car = $\dfrac{\text{distance}}{\text{time}} = \dfrac{570}{16}$

                     = 35.625 km/hr.

23. **(d)**

24. **(b)**

    Required no. of screws = 6097 × 30 = 182910

25. **(d)**

    Required value = 10000000 − 7346879

                   = 2653121

26. **(c)**

    Required mass = 14.250 × 19 = 270.75 kg

27. **(b)**

    Greater number = 9470587 + 6976583

                  = 16447170

28. **(b)**

29. **(c)**

    Required number = 3760924 + 39067

                 = 3799991

30. **(b)**

    Cost of 14 chairs = 1479 × 479 = 708441

Integers

The collection of whole numbers and all the negatives of natural numbers is called integers.
e.g., –3, –2, –1, 0, 1, 2, 3, 4, 5, 6, 8.... etc. are all integers.

Representation of Integers on the Number Line

We draw a line and fix a point almost in the middle of it. We can call it zero. We set off equal distances on the right hand side as well as on the left side of zero. On the right–hand side we label the point of division as 1,2,3,4,5, etc, while on the left–hand side these are labelled as –1, –2,–3,–4,–5, etc.

Example 1: Using number line find which integer is:

(i) 4 less than –3
(ii) 4 more than –1.

Solution:

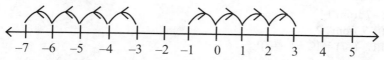

(i) 4 less than –3 = –7 [from number Line]
(ii) 4 more than –1 = 3

Example 2: Arrange the following in ascending order.

–5, –7, 0, 8, –9, 6, 7, 19, –21.

Solution: Ascending order = –21, –9, –7, –5, 0, 6, 7, 8, 19.

Absolute Value of an Integer

The absolute value of an integer is the numerical value of the integer regardless of its sign.

Or

It is the distance between the integer and zero (in units).

Operations on Integers

Addition of Integers

Rule 1. If two positive or negative numbers are added, we add their values regardless of their signs and give the sum their common sign.

Rule 2. To add a positive and a negative integer, we find the difference between their numerical values regardless of their signs and give the sign of integer with the greater value to it.

Example 3: Simplify (–212 + 322 + 33).

Solution: (322 + 33) = 355
Now, (–212) + (555) = 343

Example 4: Add (–5238) and (–2359).

Solution: (–5238) + (–2359) = – (5238 + 2359)
$$= – (7597)$$
$$= – 7597$$

Properties of Addition on Integers

(1) **Closure Property of Addition:** The sum of two integers is always an integer.

(2) **Commutative Property of Addition:** If a and b are two integers, then, a+b = b+a.

(3) **Associative Law of Addition:** If a,b and c are three integers, then a+(b+c) =(a+b)+c

(4) **Additive Inverse:** If a is an integer, then, (–a) will be additive inverse of (a)

∴ (a) + (–a) = 0

Additive Identity

The sum of any integer and zero is the number (integer) itself, i.e, If 'a' is an integer, then, a+0 = 0+a = a.

Example 5:   If a and b are integers, then, comment about x and y, if,

a +b = x+y.

Solution: ∵ (a+b) is an integer, as, 'a' and 'b' are integers,

∴ x and y should be integers [using closure property].

Subtraction of Integers

Rule: To subtract one integer from another, we take the additive inverse of the integer to be subtracted and add it to the other integer. Thus, if a and b are two integers, then, a–b = a+(–b).

Example 6:   Subtract

(i) –7 from 12.

(ii) –7 from –2

Solution: (i) 12–(–7) = 12 + [–(–7)]

= 12 + 7 = 19

(ii) –2–(–7) = –2+[–(–7)] = –2+5 = 3.

Properties of Subtraction on Integers

(1) **Closure Property:** If a and b are integers, then a –b is also an integer.

(2) **Additive/ Subtractive identity:** If a is an integer, then, a + 0 = a – 0 = a

Example 7:   The sum of two integers is –13. If one of the numbers is 2. Find the other number.

Solution: Let the other number be x.

–13 + x = 21

x = 21 –(–13)= 21+13 = 34

Multiplication of Integers

Rule 1. To Find the product of two integers with unlike signs. We find the product of their values regard less of their signs and give a minus sign to the product.

Rule 2. To find the product of two integers with same sign, we find the product of their values regardless of their signs and give a plus sign to the product.

Properties of Multiplication on Integers:

(1) **Closure Property:** The product of two integers is always an integer.

(2) **Commutative Law:** If 'a' and 'b' are two–integers then,

a × b = b × a.

(3) **Associative Law:** If 'a', 'b' and 'c' are three integers, then,

a × (b × c) = (a × b) × c.

(4) **Distributive Law:** If a,b and c are three integers then,

a × (b + c) = a × b + a × c.

(5) Multiplicative Identity: If 'a' is an integer, then,

$$a \times 1 = 1 \times a = a$$

(6) $a \times 0 = 0 \times a = 0$, if 'a' is an integer.

Example 8: Find the products:

$$(-8) \times (3) \times (7) \times (-2)$$

Solution:
$$(-8 \times 3) = -24$$
$$(7) \times (-2) = -14$$
$$\therefore -8 \times 3 \times 7 \times -2 = (-24) \times (-14)$$
$$= 224$$

Division of Integers

Rule 1. To divide one integer by another integer, with both integers having unlike signs, we denied the integers and put a (–) sign to the quotient.

Rule 2. To find the quotient of two integers with same sign we find the quotient of their values regardless of their signs and give a plus sign to the quotient.

Properties of Divisions on Integers

(i) If a and b are integers then $(a \div b)$ is not necessarily an integer.

(ii) If a is an integer and $a \neq 0$, then, $(a \div a) = 1$

(iii) If a is an integer then $(a \div 1) = a$

(iv) If a is a nonzero integer then $(0 \div a) = 0$ but $(a \div 0)$ is not defined.

(v) If a,b and c are integers then $(a \div b) \div c \neq a \div (b \div c)$, unless $c = 1$.

(vi) If a,b, and c are integers, if a >b, then,

   (a) $a \div c > b \div c$, if c is positive,

   (b) $a \div c < b \div c$, if c is negative.

Example 9: If $a > c$, and

$a \div c > b \div c$, then b will be

   (a) positive   (b) negative

   (c) zero   (d) any arbitrary number

Solution: If $a > c$, then,

$a \div b > c \div b$

If, b is positive.

Example 10: $[36 \div (-4)] + (3 \div 3) \times 7 + 3$

Solution: $(-9) + 1 \times 7 + 3$
$$= -9 + 7 + 3$$
$$= 10 - 9 = 1$$

Multiple Choice Questions

1. The additive inverse of –7 is
   (a) 7
   (b) 0
   (c) –5
   (d) –6

2. 2 less than –6 is
   (a) –8
   (b) –4
   (c) 4
   (d) None of these

3. The sum of two integers is –17. If one of them is 12 then the other is
   (a) 29
   (b) –29
   (c) –5
   (d) 5

4. The sum of two integers is 23. If one of them is –7 then the other is
   (a) –30
   (b) 16
   (c) –16
   (d) 30

5. 4 more than –7 is
   (a) –11
   (b) –3
   (c) 3
   (d) 11

6. $9 \times (-16) + (-12) \times (-16) =$?
   (a) 48
   (b) –48
   (c) 24
   (d) –54

7. $(-12) \times 7 + (-12) \times (-4) =$?
   (a) 32
   (b) –32
   (c) –36
   (d) 36

8. The sum of two integers is 65. If one of them is –47 what is the other number?
   (a) 112
   (b) –112
   (c) 18
   (d) –18

9. The difference of two integers is –27. If one of them is 32 then what is the other?
   (a) –59
   (b) 59
   (c) 5
   (d) –5

10. From the sum of 33 and –47, –84 is subtracted. What is the result?
    (a) 70
    (b) –70
    (c) 94
    (d) –94

11. $[37-(-6)] + [11-(-32)] =$?
    (a) 86
    (b) 74
    (c) –86
    (d) –74

12. The sum of two integers is –27. If one of them is 265 then what is the other?
    (a) 292
    (b) –292
    (c) 238
    (d) –238

13. Subtract the sum of –1070 and 813 from 37.
    (a) 294
    (b) –294
    (c) 272
    (d) –274

14. What is the successor of –99?
    (a) –100
    (b) –98
    (c) 100
    (d) 98

15. What is the predecessor of –79?
    (a) –78
    (b) –80
    (c) 78
    (d) 80

16. What is the sum of –23, 62, –57 & 13?
    (a) –5
    (b) 5
    (c) 15
    (d) –15

17. What is additive inverse of –100?
    (a) 100
    (b) 0
    (c) –1
    (d) 1

18. $5 + (-2) + (-7) + 6 =$?
    (a) 2
    (b) –2
    (c) 3
    (d) –3

19. $-2 + (-7) + 3 + (6) + (-9) + 11 =$?
    (a) 4
    (b) –2
    (c) 2
    (d) –4

20. If –5 is added to 12 and result is subtracted from –7. Which number is obtained?
    (a) –5
    (b) 0
    (c) 14
    (d) –14

21. Amir had ₹ 28760 in his bank account and his wife Laxmi had a debt of ₹ 12380. What was their combined net balance?
    (a) ₹ 16380
    (b) ₹ 14380
    (c) ₹ 15380
    (d) ₹ 17380

22. What is the value of $|-5 - 26 + 17|$?
    (a) –14
    (b) 14
    (c) 48
    (d) –48

23. What should be added to 57 to obtain –79?
   (a) –136
   (b) 136
   (c) –22
   (d) None of these

24. Subtract –2473 from the difference of 5396 and 7896.
   (a) 27
   (b) 4773
   (c) 4973
   (d) 4873

25. What we will get when –49 is added to the difference of 72 and –99?
   (a) 76
   (b) –76
   (c) –21
   (d) 122

26. What is the value of
   1 + (–473) + (–375) + (–383) + (–283) + 1700
   (a) 187
   (b) 287
   (c) 286
   (d) 186

27. The sum of two integers is –307. If one of them is –173 what is the other?
   (a) 134
   (b) –134
   (c) 144
   (d) –134

28. What is the value of (–705) + 487 + (–317) + 265?
   (a) 270
   (b) –270
   (c) 370
   (d) –370

29. Find the sum of predecessor of (–1709) and the successor of (–2305).
   (a) 4014
   (b) 4014
   (c) 594
   (d) None of these

30. Find the difference of negative of highest three digit number and smallest four digit number.
   (a) 1
   (b) –1999
   (c) 1999
   (d) None of these

Answer Key									
1. (a)	2. (a)	3. (b)	4. (d)	5. (b)	6. (a)	7. (c)	8. (a)	9. (b)	10 (a)
11. (a)	12. (b)	13. (a)	14. (b)	15. (b)	16. (a)	17. (a)	18. (a)	19. (c)	20. (d)
21. (a)	22. (b)	23. (a)	24. (c)	25. (d)	26. (a)	27. (b)	28. (a)	29. (b)	30. (c)

Hints _and_ Solutions

1. **(a)**

2. **(a)** $-6-2=-8$

3. **(b)** If x is other number, then $12+x=-17$

    $x=-17-12=-29$

4. **(d)** $x+(-7)=23$

    $\Rightarrow \quad x=23+7=30$

5. **(b)** $-7+4=-3$

6. **(a)** $?=9(-16)+(-12)(-16)$

    $=-144+192=48$

7. **(c)** $?=(-12)7+(-12)(-4)$

    $=-84+48=-36$

8. **(a)** $-47+x=65$

    $\Rightarrow x=65+47=112$

9. **(b)** $32-x=-27$

    $\Rightarrow \quad x=32+27=59$

10. **(a)** Required result $=[33+(-47)]-(-84)$

    $=-14+84=70$

11. **(a)** $?=[37-(-6)]+[11-(-32)]$

    $=(37+6)+(11+32)=43+43=86$

12. **(b)** $265+x=-27$

    $\Rightarrow x=-27-265=292$

13. **(a)** $37-(-1070+813)$

    $=37-(-257)=37+257=294$

14. **(b)** Successor of $-99=-99+1=-98$

15. **(b)** Predecessor of $-79=-79-1=-80$

16. **(a)** Required sum $=(-23)+62+(-57)+13$

    $=-23+62-57+13$

    $=-80+75=-5$

17. **(a)**

18. **(a)** $5-2-7+6=11-9=2$

19. **(c)** $-2-7+3+6-9+11$

    $=-18+20=2$

20. **(d)** Required result $=-7-(-5+12)$

    $=-7-7=-14$

21. **(a)** Net balance $=28760-12380=$ ₹ 16380

22. **(b)** $\left|-5-26+17\right|=\left|-31+17\right|=\left|-14\right|=14$

23. **(a)** $57+x=-79 \Rightarrow x=-79-57=-136$

24. **(c)** $(7896-5396)-(-2473)$

    $=2500+2473=4973$

25. **(d)** $-49+(72-(-99)]$

    $=-49+(72+99)$

    $=-49+171=122$

26. **(a)** Required value

    $=1701-473-375-383-283$

    $=1701-1514=187$

27. **(b)** $-173+x=-307$

    $\Rightarrow x=-307+173$

    $\Rightarrow x=-134$

28. **(a)** Required value

    $=(-705-317)+(487+265)$

    $=-1022+752=-270$

29. **(b)** Predecessor of $-1709=-1710$

    Successor of $-2305=-2304$

    $\therefore$ Sum of -1710 & $-2304=-4014$

30. **(c)** Required difference

    $1000-(-999)=1000+999=1999$

4   Fractions

Fraction

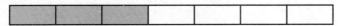

In the above figure a strip is divided into 7 equal parts, out of which 3 is shaded. The shaded portion represents three-sevenths.

In numeral, it is written as $\dfrac{3}{7}$.

$\dfrac{3}{7}$ is a fractions

Here, 3 is called numerator and 7 is called denominator.

In proper fraction, numerator < denominator.

Types of Fractions

Proper Fraction

A fraction whose numerator is less than its denominator is called a proper fraction.

Example: $\dfrac{1}{3}, \dfrac{2}{7}, \dfrac{5}{9}$ etc.

Improper Fraction

A fraction whose numerator is greater than or equal to its denominator is called an improper fraction.

Example: $\dfrac{5}{4}, \dfrac{7}{3}, \dfrac{25}{6}$ etc.

Mixed Fraction

A combination of a whole number and a proper fraction is called a mixed fraction.

Example: $7\dfrac{1}{2}, 5\dfrac{2}{3}, 4\dfrac{5}{7}$ etc.

Example 1:   What fraction of a day is 6 hours?

   Solution: 1 day = 24 hours.

$$\therefore \text{Fraction} = \frac{6}{24} = \frac{1}{4}$$

Example 2:   What fraction of a year is 17 days.

   Solution: 1 year = 365 days

$$\therefore \text{Fraction} = \frac{17}{365}$$

Example 3: Write three improper fractions with denominator 5.

Solution: Three improper fractions with denominator 5 are $\dfrac{7}{5}, \dfrac{8}{5}, \dfrac{11}{5}$

Example 4: Fill up the blanks with >, < or = .

(i) $\dfrac{3}{7} \square 1$ (ii) $\dfrac{7}{3} \square 2$ (iii) $\dfrac{17}{17} \square 1$

Solution:

(i) $\dfrac{3}{7} \square 1$

$\because \ 3 < 7$

$\therefore \ \dfrac{3}{7} < 1$

(ii) $\dfrac{7}{3} \square 2$

$\because \ 7 > 6$

$\therefore \ \dfrac{7}{3} > 2$

(iii) $\dfrac{17}{17} \boxed{=} 1$

$17 = 17$

Equivalent Fraction

Two or more fractions representing the same part of a whole number are known as equivalent fraction.

Example: $\dfrac{2}{5} = \dfrac{4}{10} = \dfrac{4}{35}$

Example 5: Write three fractions equivalent to $\dfrac{3}{11}$.

Solution: $\dfrac{3}{11} = \dfrac{6}{22} = \dfrac{15}{55} = \dfrac{24}{88}$

Example 6: Write a fraction equivalent to $\dfrac{5}{8}$ with denominator 56.

Solution: $\dfrac{5}{8} = \dfrac{5 \times 7}{8 \times 7} = \dfrac{35}{56}$

Like Fraction

The fractions having the same denominator are called like fractions.

Example: $\dfrac{1}{9}, \dfrac{2}{9}, \dfrac{4}{9}, \dfrac{5}{9}$

Unlike Fraction

Fractions whose denominators are different, are called unlike fractions.

Example: $\frac{1}{3}, \frac{2}{5}, \frac{7}{8}$ etc.

Example 7: Convert the following into like fractions $\frac{1}{2}, \frac{2}{3}, \frac{4}{5}, \frac{3}{7}$.

Solution: Here, LCM of 2, 3, 5, 7 = 210

$$\frac{1}{2} = \frac{1 \times 105}{2 \times 105} = \frac{105}{210}$$

$$\frac{2}{3} = \frac{2 \times 70}{3 \times 70} = \frac{140}{210}$$

$$\frac{4}{5} = \frac{4 \times 42}{5 \times 42} = \frac{168}{210}$$

$$\frac{3}{7} = \frac{3 \times 30}{7 \times 30} = \frac{90}{210}$$

$\frac{105}{210}, \frac{140}{210}, \frac{168}{210}, \frac{90}{210}$ are like fractions.

Cross Multiplication of Fraction

If $\frac{a}{b}$ and $\frac{c}{d}$ are two fractions then

$$\frac{a}{b} \diagup\!\!\!\!\diagdown \frac{c}{d}$$

or $ad = bc$

If $ad > bc$ then $\frac{a}{b} > \frac{c}{d}$.

If $ad < bc$ then $\frac{a}{b} < \frac{c}{d}$.

If $ad = bc$ then $\frac{a}{b} = \frac{c}{d}$.

Example 8: Arrange the fractions $\frac{2}{3}, \frac{1}{6}, \frac{5}{9}, \frac{7}{12}$ in descending order.

Solution: LCM of 3, 6, 9, 12 = 36.

$\therefore \frac{2}{3} = \frac{2 \times 12}{3 \times 12} = \frac{24}{36}$; $\frac{1}{6} = \frac{1 \times 6}{6 \times 6} = \frac{6}{36}$

$\frac{5}{9} = \frac{5 \times 4}{9 \times 4} = \frac{20}{36}$; $\frac{7}{12} = \frac{7 \times 3}{12 \times 3} = \frac{21}{36}$

$\frac{24}{36} > \frac{21}{36} > \frac{20}{36} > \frac{6}{36}$

$\therefore$ Descending order is $\frac{2}{3} > \frac{7}{12} > \frac{5}{9} > \frac{1}{6}$

Example 9: Solve $\dfrac{2}{3} + 3\dfrac{1}{6} + 4\dfrac{2}{9} + 2$.

Solution: Here, $\dfrac{2}{3} + \dfrac{19}{6} + \dfrac{38}{9} + 2$

$$= \dfrac{12 + 57 + 76 + 36}{18} = \dfrac{181}{18} = 10\dfrac{1}{18}$$

Example 10: Simplify $8 - 3\dfrac{1}{2} - 2\dfrac{1}{4}$.

Solution: We have $8 - \dfrac{7}{2} - \dfrac{9}{4}$

$$= \dfrac{32 - 14 - 9}{4} = \dfrac{32 - 23}{4} = \dfrac{9}{4}$$

$$= 2\dfrac{1}{4}$$

Example 11: Of $\dfrac{3}{4}$ and $\dfrac{5}{7}$ which is greater and by how much?

Solution:

$\qquad \dfrac{3}{4} \qquad\qquad \dfrac{5}{7}$

$\qquad 3 \times 7 \qquad\quad 4 \times 5$

$\qquad 21 \qquad > \qquad 20$

$\Rightarrow \dfrac{3}{4} > \dfrac{5}{7}$

$= \dfrac{21 - 20}{28} = \dfrac{1}{28}$

Example 12: A piece of wire $3\dfrac{1}{4}$ m long broke into two prices. One piece is $\dfrac{7}{8}$ m long. How long is the other piece?

Solution: Here, required length $= 3\dfrac{1}{4} - \dfrac{7}{8}$

$$= \dfrac{13}{4} - \dfrac{7}{8}$$

$$= \dfrac{26 - 7}{8} = \dfrac{19}{8} = 2\dfrac{3}{8} \text{ m}$$

1. The smallest of the fractions $\frac{3}{4}, \frac{1}{2}, \frac{5}{6}, \frac{2}{3}$ is

   (a) $\frac{1}{2}$

   (b) $\frac{3}{4}$

   (c) $\frac{3}{4}$

   (d) $\frac{5}{6}$

2. The largest of the fraction $\frac{2}{3}, \frac{3}{4}, \frac{5}{6}, \frac{7}{12}$ is

   (a) $\frac{1}{2}$

   (b) $\frac{3}{4}$

   (c) $\frac{3}{4}$

   (d) $\frac{5}{6}$

3. If $\frac{5}{6}$ is equivalent to $\frac{X}{24}$, then what is the value of X?

   (a) 15

   (b) 20

   (c) 25

   (d) 30

4. Which of the following is a proper fraction?

   (a) $\frac{4}{3}$

   (b) $\frac{6}{5}$

   (c) $1\frac{2}{3}$

   (d) $2\frac{3}{4}$

5. A fraction equivalent to $\frac{57}{95}$ is

   (a) $\frac{3}{5}$

   (b) $\frac{3}{7}$

   (c) $\frac{3}{5}$

   (d) None of these

6. A fraction equivalent to $\frac{2}{3}$ is

   (a) $\frac{2+3}{3+3}$

   (b) $\frac{2-1}{3-1}$

   (c) $\frac{2 \times 3}{3 \times 3}$

   (d) $\frac{2 \div 3}{3 \div 4}$

7. What should be added to $9\frac{2}{3}$ to get 19?

   (a) $9\frac{1}{3}$

   (b) $9\frac{2}{3}$

   (c) $8\frac{1}{3}$

   (d) $9\frac{1}{2}$

8. Which of the following is not a proper fraction?

   (a) $\frac{3}{4}$

   (b) $\frac{7}{8}$

   (c) $\frac{6}{11}$

   (d) $\frac{8}{5}$

9. Raju bought $7\frac{1}{2}$ litres of milk. Out of this milk $5\frac{3}{4}$ litres was consumed. How much milk is left with him?

   (a) $1\frac{3}{4}$ litre

   (b) $1\frac{1}{4}$ litre

   (c) $1\frac{1}{3}$ litre

   (d) None of these

10. What is the value of $6\frac{1}{2} - 5\frac{2}{3} + 3\frac{1}{4}$?

    (a) $1\frac{11}{12}$

    (b) $4\frac{1}{12}$

    (c) $3\frac{1}{12}$

    (d) $5\frac{1}{12}$

11. What is the value of $5 - \frac{2}{3} - \frac{3}{4}$?

    (a) $4\frac{7}{12}$

    (b) $2\frac{7}{12}$

    (c) $3\frac{7}{12}$

    (d) None of these

12. What is the difference of $\frac{21}{24}$ and $\frac{10}{24}$?

(a) $\frac{11}{12}$

(b) $\frac{11}{16}$

(c) $\frac{11}{24}$

(d) None of these

13. What value is obtained when $1\frac{5}{6}$ is subtracted from 8?

(a) $5\frac{1}{6}$

(b) $6\frac{1}{6}$

(c) $3\frac{1}{6}$

(d) $7\frac{1}{6}$

14. What is the equivalent fraction of $\frac{3}{5}$ having numerator 21?

(a) $\frac{21}{34}$

(b) $\frac{21}{63}$

(c) $\frac{21}{49}$

(d) $\frac{21}{35}$

15. What is the equivalent fraction of $\frac{5}{12}$ having denominator 84?

(a) $\frac{25}{84}$

(b) $\frac{35}{84}$

(c) $\frac{30}{84}$

(d) $\frac{40}{84}$

16. What is the equivalent fraction of $\frac{56}{70}$ with numerator 4?

(a) $\frac{4}{15}$

(b) $\frac{4}{6}$

(c) $\frac{4}{5}$

(d) $\frac{4}{7}$

17. What of the following is correct?

(a) $\frac{2}{3} > \frac{5}{6}$

(b) $\frac{4}{5} > \frac{2}{3}$

(c) $\frac{5}{7} < \frac{2}{3}$

(d) $\frac{6}{7} < \frac{4}{5}$

18. What of the following is not correct?

(a) $\frac{2}{5} > \frac{1}{3}$

(b) $\frac{1}{4} > \frac{2}{3}$

(c) $\frac{4}{5} < \frac{6}{7}$

(d) $\frac{1}{7} > \frac{3}{5}$

19. A piece of wire is $3\frac{3}{4}$ m long broke into two pieces. One piece is $\frac{5}{8}$ m long, then what is the length of other piece?

(a) $2\frac{1}{8}$

(b) $3\frac{1}{8}$

(c) $4\frac{1}{8}$

(d) None of these

20. What should be added to $9\frac{2}{3}$ to get 40?

(a) $32\frac{1}{3}$

(b) $28\frac{1}{3}$

(c) $30\frac{1}{3}$

(d) $31\frac{1}{3}$

21. $3 + 1\frac{1}{5} - 2\frac{1}{3} + 2\frac{1}{5} = ?$

(a) $5\frac{1}{15}$

(b) $2\frac{1}{15}$

(c) $3\frac{1}{15}$

(d) $4\frac{1}{15}$

22. $5 - \frac{1}{2} + \frac{1}{3} - \frac{1}{4} = ?$

(a) $4\frac{7}{12}$

(b) $3\frac{7}{12}$

(c) $2\frac{7}{12}$

(d) $5\frac{7}{12}$

23. $7 + \frac{1}{5} - 2\frac{1}{3} + 4\frac{1}{2} = ?$

(a) $7\frac{11}{30}$

(b) $9\frac{11}{30}$

(c) $8\frac{11}{30}$

(d) $6\frac{11}{30}$

24. What of the following is correct?

   (a) $1\frac{1}{5} < 1\frac{1}{2} < 1\frac{3}{5} < 1\frac{3}{4}$

   (b) $2\frac{1}{2} < 2\frac{1}{4} < 2\frac{1}{5} < 2\frac{1}{8}$

   (c) $\frac{2}{3} < \frac{1}{2} < \frac{1}{4} < \frac{3}{4}$

   (d) None of these

25. What should be added to   – to get $8\frac{1}{2}$?

   (a) $1\frac{5}{6}$

   (b) $2\frac{5}{6}$

   (c) –

   (d) $1\frac{1}{3}$

26. What should be subtracted from 5 to get $3\frac{2}{5}$?

   (a) $1\frac{2}{5}$

   (b) $1\frac{3}{5}$

   (c) $2\frac{2}{5}$

   (d) $2\frac{3}{5}$

27. $8\frac{1}{3} - 7\frac{2}{5} + 4\frac{2}{3} - 6\frac{1}{5} = ?$

   (a) $\frac{3}{5}$

   (b) $-\frac{3}{5}$

   (c) $\frac{2}{5}$

   (d) $-\frac{2}{5}$

28. $14 - \left[12 - \left\{9 - \left(7 - \overline{6 - 2}\right)\right\}\right] = ?$

   (a) 6

   (b) 8

   (c) 7

   (d) 10

29. $\left[5\frac{1}{7} - \left\{3\frac{3}{10} + \left(2\frac{4}{5} - \frac{7}{10}\right)\right\}\right]$

   (a) $\frac{9}{35}$

   (b) $-\frac{9}{35}$

   (c) $\frac{3}{35}$

   (d) $-\frac{3}{35}$

30. $\frac{3}{4}$ of $\left(\frac{2}{3} - \frac{3}{5}\right) + \frac{1}{2} \times \frac{2}{3} = ?$

   (a) $\frac{1}{5}$

   (b) $1\frac{1}{5}$

   (c) $\frac{2}{5}$

   (d) $2\frac{1}{5}$

Answer Key

1. (a)	2. (b)	3. (b)	4. (a)	5. (c)	6. (c)	7. (a)	8. (d)	9. (a)	10 (b)
11. (c)	12. (c)	13. (b)	14. (d)	15. (b)	16. (c)	17. (b)	18. (d)	19. (b)	20. (c)
21. (d)	22. (a)	23. (b)	24. (a)	25. (a)	26. (b)	27. (b)	28. (b)	29. (b)	30. (c)

Hints and Solutions

1. **(a)** Here, LCM of 4, 2, 6, 3 = 12.

$$\frac{3}{4}=\frac{9}{12};\ \frac{1}{2}=\frac{6}{12};\ \frac{5}{6}=\frac{10}{12};\ \frac{2}{3}=\frac{8}{12}$$

$$\therefore \frac{6}{12}<\frac{8}{12}<\frac{9}{12}<\frac{10}{12}$$

Hence, $\dfrac{1}{2}<\dfrac{2}{3}<\dfrac{3}{4}<\dfrac{5}{6}$

2. **(b)** LCM of 3, 4, 6, 12 = 12

$$\frac{2}{3}=\frac{8}{12};\ \frac{3}{4}=\frac{9}{12};\ \frac{5}{6}=\frac{10}{12};\ \frac{7}{12}=\frac{7}{12}$$

$$\therefore \frac{7}{12}<\frac{8}{12}<\frac{9}{12}<\frac{10}{12}$$

$$\Rightarrow \frac{7}{12}<\frac{2}{3}<\frac{3}{4}<\frac{5}{6}$$

3. **(b)** Given $\dfrac{X}{24}=\dfrac{5}{6}\Rightarrow X=\dfrac{24\times 5}{6}=20$

4. **(a)**

5. **(c)** $\dfrac{57}{95}=\dfrac{3}{5}$

6. **(c)**

7. **(a)** Required value

$$=19-\frac{29}{3}=\frac{57-29}{3}=\frac{28}{3}=9\frac{1}{3}$$

8. **(d)**

9. **(a)** Required amount of milk

$$=\frac{15}{2}-\frac{23}{4}=\frac{30-23}{4}=\frac{7}{4}=1\frac{3}{4}\text{ litre}$$

10. **(b)** $6\dfrac{1}{2}-5\dfrac{2}{3}+3\dfrac{1}{4}$

$$=\frac{13}{2}-\frac{17}{3}+\frac{13}{4}=\frac{78-69+39}{12}$$

$$=\frac{49}{12}=48\frac{1}{12}$$

11. **(c)** Required value =

$$5-\frac{2}{3}-\frac{3}{4}=\frac{60-8-9}{12}=\frac{60-17}{12}$$

$$=\frac{43}{12}=3\frac{7}{12}$$

12. **(c)** Required value $=\dfrac{7}{8}-\dfrac{5}{12}=\dfrac{21-10}{24}=\dfrac{11}{24}$

13. **(b)** Required value =

$$8-\frac{11}{6}=\frac{48-11}{6}=\frac{37}{6}=6\frac{1}{6}$$

14. **(d)** $\dfrac{3}{5}=\dfrac{3\times 7}{5\times 7}=\dfrac{21}{35}$

15. **(b)** $\dfrac{5}{12}=\dfrac{5\times 7}{12\times 7}=\dfrac{35}{84}$

16. **(c)** $\dfrac{56}{70}=\dfrac{4}{5}$

17. **(b)** $\dfrac{4}{5}>\dfrac{2}{3}\Rightarrow 12>10$

18. **(d)** $\dfrac{2}{5}>\dfrac{1}{3}\Rightarrow 6>5$

$$\frac{1}{4}>\frac{2}{3}\Rightarrow 3>8$$

$$\frac{4}{5}<\frac{6}{7}\Rightarrow 28<30$$

$$\frac{1}{7}>\frac{3}{5}\Rightarrow 5>21\ \text{(Not correct)}$$

19. **(b)** Required length =

$$\frac{15}{4}-\frac{5}{8}=\frac{30-5}{8}=\frac{25}{8}=3\frac{1}{8}$$

20. **(c)** Here,

$$40-\frac{29}{3}=\frac{120-29}{3}=\frac{91}{3}=30\frac{1}{3}$$

21. **(d)** $?=3+\dfrac{6}{5}-\dfrac{7}{3}+\dfrac{11}{5}=\dfrac{45+18-35+33}{15}$

$$=\frac{61}{15}=4\frac{1}{15}$$

22. **(a)** $5 - \dfrac{1}{2} + \dfrac{1}{3} - \dfrac{1}{4} = \dfrac{60 - 6 + 4 - 3}{12} = \dfrac{64 - 9}{12}$

$$= \dfrac{55}{12} = 4\dfrac{7}{12}$$

23. **(b)** $? = 7 + \dfrac{1}{5} - \dfrac{7}{3} + \dfrac{9}{2}$

$$= \dfrac{210 + 6 - 70 + 135}{30} = \dfrac{351 - 70}{30} = \dfrac{281}{30}$$

$$= 9\dfrac{11}{30}$$

24. **(a)**

$$\dfrac{6}{5} < \dfrac{3}{2} < \dfrac{8}{5} < \dfrac{7}{4}$$

25. **(a)**

$$\dfrac{17}{2} - \dfrac{20}{3} = \dfrac{51 - 40}{6} = \dfrac{11}{6} = 1\dfrac{5}{6}$$

26. **(b)**

$$5 - \dfrac{17}{5} = \dfrac{25 - 17}{5} = \dfrac{8}{5} = 1\dfrac{3}{5}$$

27. **(b)**

$$8\dfrac{1}{3} - 7\dfrac{2}{5} + 4\dfrac{2}{3} - 6\dfrac{1}{5}$$

$$= \dfrac{25}{3} - \dfrac{37}{5} + \dfrac{14}{3} - \dfrac{31}{5}$$

$$= \dfrac{125 - 111 + 70 - 93}{15}$$

$$= \dfrac{195 - 204}{15}$$

$$= \dfrac{-9}{15} = \dfrac{-3}{5}$$

28. **(b)**

Required expression

$= 14 - [12 - \{9 - (7 - \overline{6 - 2})\}]$

$= 14 - [12 - \{9 - (7 - 4)\}]$

$= 14 - [12 - \{9 - 3\}]$

$= 14 - [12 - 6]$

$= 14 - 6 = 8$

29. **(b)** Given expression

$$= \left[\dfrac{36}{7} - \left\{\dfrac{33}{10} + \left(\dfrac{14}{5} - \dfrac{7}{10}\right)\right\}\right]$$

$$= \left[\dfrac{36}{7} - \left\{\dfrac{33}{10} + \left(\dfrac{28 - 7}{10}\right)\right\}\right]$$

$$= \left[\dfrac{36}{7} - \left\{\dfrac{33}{10} + \dfrac{21}{10}\right\}\right]$$

$$= \dfrac{36}{7} - \dfrac{54}{10}$$

$$= \dfrac{360 - 378}{70} = \dfrac{-18}{70} = \dfrac{-9}{35}$$

30. **(c)**

$$? = \dfrac{3}{4} \, of \left(\dfrac{2}{3} - \dfrac{2}{5}\right) + \dfrac{1}{2} \div \dfrac{5}{2}$$

$$= \dfrac{3}{4} \, of \left(\dfrac{10 - 6}{15}\right) + \dfrac{1}{2} \div \dfrac{5}{2}$$

$$= \dfrac{3}{4} \, of \, \dfrac{4}{15} + \dfrac{1}{2} \div \dfrac{5}{2}$$

$$= \dfrac{1}{5} + \dfrac{1}{2} \times \dfrac{2}{5}$$

$$= \dfrac{1}{5} + \dfrac{1}{5} = \dfrac{2}{5}$$

Decimal

A decimal is just another way to write a fraction. In the fractions, we express a number in $\left(\dfrac{p}{q}\right)$ form. The fractions whose denominator are 10,100,1000 etc., are called decimal fractions.

e.g., $\dfrac{6}{10}, \dfrac{25}{100}, \dfrac{3}{1000}$, etc.

$\dfrac{1}{10}$ is expressed as one-tenths.

$\dfrac{1}{100}$ is expressed as one-hundredths.

$\dfrac{1}{1000}$ is expressed as one-thousandths.

Like and Unlike Decimals

Decimal having the same number of decimal places are known as like decimals and decimals having different number of decimal places are called unlike decimals.

Like decimals are 2.03, 3.72, 5.63, 2.78, as these numbers have 2 digits after decimal, i.e, two decimal places.

Unlike decimals are, 3.73, 5.723. as these numbers have different number of digits after decimal.

Example 1: Are 5.73, 2.232, 5.1, 6, like decimals. If not so, convert them into like decimals.

   Solution: ∵ number of decimal places in 5.73, 2.232, 5.1 and 6 are different.

                   ∴ these are not like decimals.

                   For converting these decimals into like decimals, we will put suitable number of zeros after decimal places.

                   5.73 = 5.730

                   2.232 = 2.232

                   5.1 = 5.100

                   6 = 6.000

Example 2: Write 6.235 in expanded form.

   Solution: 6.235 = 6 + 0.200 + 0.030 + 0.005

                $= 6 + \dfrac{2}{10} + \dfrac{3}{100} + \dfrac{5}{1000}$

Conversion of a Decimal into a Fractional Number

Example 3: Convert the following decimals to fractional form

               (a)   624.21

               (b)   221.324

Solution:

$$(a)\ 624.21 = 624 + 0.21$$

$$= 624 + \frac{21}{100}$$

$$= \frac{62421}{100}$$

$$(b)\ 221.324 = \frac{221324}{1000}$$

Example 4: Write 102.23 in words.

Solution: 102.23 can be expressed as one hundred two point two three.

Conversion of a Fractional Number to Decimal

Example 5: Convert the following fractions into decimals

(a) $\dfrac{64659}{100}$ (b) $3\dfrac{2}{7}$

(c) $\dfrac{61}{8}$ (d) $\dfrac{18}{25}$

Solution:

(a) $\dfrac{64659}{100} = 646.59$

(b) $3\dfrac{2}{7} = 3 + \dfrac{2}{7} = 3 + 0.28$

$$= 3.28$$

(c) $\dfrac{61}{8} = \dfrac{56+5}{8} = 7 + \dfrac{5}{8}$

$$= 7 + 0.625 = 7.625$$

(d) $\dfrac{18}{25} = \dfrac{18 \times 4}{25 \times 4} = \dfrac{72}{100} = 0.72$

Comparison of Decimal

Working Rule

(1) Convert the given decimals into like decimals.

(2) Compare the whole number part. The greater the whole number, greater is the decimal.

(3) If the whole number part is same, then compare the digits after decimal.

Example 6: Which is greater 78.4, 78.6, or 78.618?

Solution: 78.4 = 78.400

78.6 = 78.600

78.618 = 78.618

∵ The whole number part i.e, 78 is same.

Now comparing the latter part.

400 < 600 < 618

∴ 78.400 < 78.600 < 78.61

∴ 78.4 < 78.6 < 78.618

Decimals

Example 7: Arrange the following decimals into ascending order.

5.13, 3.27, 1.732, 5.32

Solution: Comparing whole number part, we have,

5.32, 5.13, > 3.27> 1.732

But we have to compare between 5.32 and 5.13

Comparing the latter part of decimal, we have,

32 > 13

∴ 5.32 > 5.13

∴ 5.32 > 5.13 > 3.27 > 1.732

Uses of Decimals in Our Daily Life

1. **Money:** We know that,

    1 rupee = 100 paise,

    ∴ 1 paisa = $\dfrac{1}{100}$ rupee = 0.01 rupee.

    For example: Writing 2874 paise in rupees will be $28 + 74 \times 0.01 = 28.74$ rupees.

2. **Measurement of Length:**

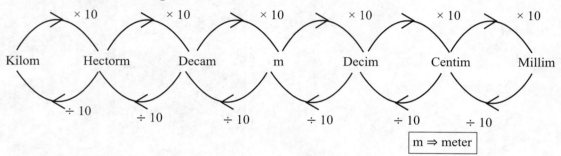

1 kilometer = 1000 m

$\Rightarrow 1m = \dfrac{1}{1000}$ km = 0.001km

$\Rightarrow 1$ mm = $\dfrac{1}{1000}$ = 0.001 m

$\Rightarrow 1$ cm = $\dfrac{1}{100}$ m = 0.01m

3. **Measurement of Weights:**

    $1 g = \dfrac{1}{1000}$ kg = 0.001 kg

    $1 mg = \dfrac{1}{1000}$ g = 0.001 g

4. **Measurement of Capacities:**

    1 kl = 1000 l ⇒ 1 l = 0.001 kl

    1 ml = $\dfrac{1}{1000}l$ ⇒ 1 ml = 0.001 l

Example 8: Convert 35 *l* 24 m*l* into litre.

Solution: 1 ml = $\dfrac{1}{1000}$ l = 0.001 l

$\therefore$ 24ml = 24 × $\dfrac{1}{1000}$ l = 0.024 *l*

$\therefore$ 35 l 24 ml = 35.024 *l*

Operation on Decimal Numbers

Addition: Convert the decimals into like decimals. Write the decimals in columns keeping decimal point of each decimal in the same column. Then follow the procedure of addition. Subtraction is done in a similar fashion.

Example 9: Add 5.24, 3.648 and 2.684.

Solution:

$$
\begin{array}{r}
5.24 = 5.240 \\
3.648 = 3.648 \\
2.684 = 2.684 \\
+ \qquad + \\
\hline
\text{Sum} = 11.572
\end{array}
$$

Example 10: Subtract 9.32 from 1000.

Solution:

$$
\begin{array}{r}
1000 = 1000.00 \\
9.32 = 0009.32 \\
- \qquad - \\
\hline
\text{Difference} = 990.68
\end{array}
$$

Example 11: A student named Radha scored 14.6 marks more than her classmate Krishna. If the marks scored by Radha is 21, then calculate the marks secured by Krishna.

Solution:

Marks scored by Radha = 21

$\therefore$ Marks scored by Krishna

$\qquad$ = 21 – 14.6

$\qquad$ = 6.4

1. Which of the following is the correct order
   (a) $5.5 < 5.05 < 5.005 < 5.555$
   (b) $5.005 < 5.05 < 5.5 < 5.555$
   (c) $5.05 < 5.55 < 5.005 < 5.555$
   (d) None of these

2. $0.4 + 0.004 + 4.4 = ?$
   (a) 5.2   (b) 5.404
   (c) 4.804   (d) 4.444

3. $1.103 - 0.3 = ?$
   (a) 0.803   (b) 0.83
   (c) 0.38   (d) 1.03

4. $3 - 0.007 = ?$
   (a) 2.933   (b) 2.093
   (c) 2.903   (d) 2.993

5. Among 7.6, 7.006, 7.66 and 7.08, which is the largest number?
   (a) 7.08   (b) 7.66
   (c) 7.6   (d) 7.006

6. $8 + \dfrac{3}{10} + \dfrac{4}{100} + \dfrac{7}{1000}$
   (a) 8.347   (b) 8.0347
   (c) 8.3047   (d) 8.30047

7. $7\dfrac{1}{25} = ?$
   (a) 7.4   (b) 7.04
   (c) 7.004   (d) None of these

8. $6 - 0.23 + 1.2 - 5.76 = ?$
   (a) 1.21   (b) −1.21
   (c) 0.73   (d) 0.21

9. $37 - 35.79 = ?$
   (a) 1.31   (b) 1.21
   (c) 2.21   (d) 2.31

10. What is to be added to 74.5 to get 81?
    (a) 5.5   (b) 7.5
    (c) 6.5   (d) 7.5

11. What is to be subtracted from 7.3 to get 0.867?
    (a) 5.433   (b) 6.433
    (c) 7.433   (d) 6.233

12. By how much should 79.5 be decreased to get 27.89 ?
    (a) 53.61   (b) 52.61
    (c) 51.61   (d) 51.81

13. By how much should 32.754 by increased to get 53?
    (a) 20.246   (b) 20.346
    (c) 21.246   (d) 21.746

14. $76.3 - 7.666 - 6.77 - 5.55 = ?$
    (a) 56.341   (b) 56.314
    (c) 54.641   (d) 54.341

15. 37 mm = ?
    (a) 0.37 cm   (b) 0.037 m
    (c) 0.0037 m   (d) 0.307 cm

16. 2 kg 57 g = ?
    (a) 2.57 kg   (b) 2.570 kg
    (c) 2.057 kg   (d) None of these

17. During three days of a week, an auto driver earns ₹ 302.80, ₹ 379.20 and ₹ 297.60 respectively. What is his total earning during these days?
    (a) ₹ 979.60   (b) ₹ 978.60
    (c) ₹ 969.60   (d) ₹ 997.60

18. What is the decimal equivalent of $15\dfrac{17}{40}$?
    (a) 15.325   (b) 15.425
    (c) 15.375   (d) 15.725

19. Mohan purchased 5 kg 75 g of fruits and 3kg 465g of vegetables and put them in a bag. If this bag with these contents weights 9 kg. What is the weight of empty bag?
    (a) 465 g   (b) 480 g
    (c) 470 g   (d) 460 g

20. What should be subtracted from the sum of 4.902 & 15.376 to get 16.307 ?
    (a) 3.791   (b) 3.971
    (c) 2.971   (d) 4.971

21. If the school bag of Sanjay and Rajesh weigh 6kg 40g and 7kg 207g respectively. By how much Rajesh's bag is heavier than that of Sanjay?
    (a) 1 kg 167 g   (b) 1 kg 187 g
    (c) 2 kg 167 g   (d) 1 kg 197 g

22. Which of the following is not in correct order?
    (a) 3.72 > 3.67 > 3.05 > 3.03
    (b) 1.08 < 1.18 < 1.184
    (c) 3.502 > 3.067 > 3.126
    (d) 5.40 > 5.37 > 5.306

23. The correct expanded form of 3.07 is
    (a) $(3 \times 10) + \left(7 \times \dfrac{1}{10}\right)$

    (b) $(3 \times 1) + \left(7 \times \dfrac{1}{10}\right)$

    (c) $(3 \times 1) + \left(7 \times \dfrac{1}{100}\right)$

    (d) None of these

24. Rasmi bought 2m 5cm cloth for her salwar and 3m 35cm cloth for her shirt. What is the total length of cloth bought by her?
    (a) 5m 40cm   (b) 5m 45cm
    (c) 5m 35cm   (d) None of these

25. The distance between Suman's house and office is 17km. She covers 9km 65m by scooter 4 km 75m by bus and rest on foot. How much distance she cover by walking?
    (a) 3 km 960 m   (b) 2km 860 m
    (c) 4km 860 m   (d) 3km 860 m

26. What number we get when subtract 29.13 from 73?
    (a) 42.87   (b) 43.87
    (c) 43.97   (d) None of these

27. Ritesh purchased a book worth ₹ 447.85 from a book seller and gave him a 1000 rupee note. How much balance did he get back?
    (a) ₹ 552.25   (b) ₹ 553.15
    (c) ₹ 552.15   (d) ₹ 551.15

28. Raman has ₹ 2000. He has invested ₹ 439.75 in schoolfees, ₹ 208.75 for auto fair, ₹ 524.25 in books and rest for fooding. What is the cost of fooding?
    (a) ₹ 817.25   (b) ₹ 837.25
    (c) ₹ 827.25   (d) None of these

Answer Key

1. (b)	2. (c)	3. (a)	4. (d)	5. (b)	6. (a)	7. (b)	8. (a)	9. (b)	10 (c)
11. (b)	12. (c)	13. (a)	14. (b)	15. (b)	16. (c)	17. (a)	18. (b)	19. (d)	20. (b)
21. (a)	22. (d)	23. (c)	24. (a)	25. (d)	26. (b)	27. (c)	28. (c)		

1. **(b)**

2. **(c)** Here,
   ? = 0.4 + 0.004 + 4.4 = 4.804

3. **(a)**
   ? = 1.103 − 0.3 = 0.803

4. **(d)**
   ? = 3 − 0.007 = 2.993

5. **(b)**
   ∵ 7.006 < 7.08 < 7.6 < 7.66
   ∴ 7.66 is the largest number

6. **(a)**
   Given expression can be written as
   8 + 0.3 + 0.04 + 0.007 = 8.347

7. **(b)**
   We have $7\dfrac{1}{25} = 7 + \dfrac{1}{25} = 7.04$

8. **(a)**
   ? = 6 − 0.23 + 1.2 − 5.76
   = 7.2 − 5.99 = 1.21

9. **(b)**
   ? = 37 − 35.79 = 1.21

10. **(c)**
    Required number = 81 − 74.5 = 6.5

11. **(b)**
    Required number = 7.3 − 0.867 = 6.433

12. **(c)**
    Required number = 79.5 − 27.89 = 51.61

13. **(a)**
    Required number = 53 − 32.754 = 20.246

14. **(b)**
    ? = 76.3 − 7.666 − 6.77 − 5.55
    = 76.3 − 19.986 = 56.314

15. **(b)**
    Here, 37 mm = $\dfrac{37}{10}$ = 3.7 cm

    and 3.7 cm = $\dfrac{3.7}{100}$ = 0.037 m

16. **(c)**
    2 kg 57 g = 2 × 1000 + 57 = 2057 g
    and $\dfrac{2057}{1000}$ = 2.057 kg

17. **(a)**
    Total earning = 302.80 + 379.20 + 297.60
    = 979.60

18. **(b)**
    We have $15\dfrac{17}{40} = 15 + \dfrac{17}{40} = 15 + 0.425$
    = 15.425

19. **(d)**
    Here, 5kg 75g + 3kg 465g = 8kg 540g
    ∴ 9kg − 8kg 540g = 460g

20. **(b)**
    Here, 4.902 + 15.376 = 20.278
    then 20.278 − 16.307 = 3.971

21. **(a)**
    7kg 207g − 6kg 40g = 1kg 167g

22. **(d)**

23. **(c)**

24. **(a)**
    Total length of cloth = 2m 5cm + 3m 35cm
    = 5m 40cm

25. **(d)**
    Required distance
    = 17 − (9km 65m + 4km 75m)
    = 17 − (13 km 140 m)
    = 3km 860m

26. **(b)**
    Required number = 73 − 29.13 = 43.87

27. **(c)**
    Required balance = 1000 − 447.85 = ₹ 552.15

28. **(c)**
    Cost of fooding
    = 2000 − (439.75 + 208.75 + 524.25)
    = 2000 − 1172.75
    = 827.25

6 Simplification

In simplification of an expression there are certain laws which should be strictly adhered to. These laws are as follows:

'BODMAS' Rule

This rule depicts the correct sequence in which the operations are to be executed, so as to find out the value of a given expression.

Here,

B - Bracket,
O - of,
D - Division,
M - Multiplication,
A - Addition, and
S - Subtraction

Thus, in simplifying an expression, first of all the brackets must be removed, strictly in the order ( ), { } and [ ].

After removing the brackets, we must use the following operations strictly in the order of:

- ❏ Division
- ❏ Multiplication
- ❏ Addition
- ❏ Subtraction

Modulus of a Real Number

Modulus of a real number a is defined as

$$|a| = \begin{cases} a, & \text{if } a > 0 \\ -a, & \text{if } a < 0 \end{cases}$$

Thus, $|5| = 5$ and $|-5| = -(-5) = 5$

Virnaculum Bar

When an expression contains virnaculum, before applying the 'BODMAS' rule, we simplify the expression under the virnaculum.

Multiple Choice Questions

1. David gets on an elevator at the 11th floor of a building and rides up at the rate of 57 floors per minute. At the same time, Albert gets on an elevator at the 51st floor of the same building and rides down at the rate of 63 floors per minute. If they continue travelling at these rates, then at which floor will their paths cross?
   (a) 19   (b) 28
   (c) 30   (d) 37

2. $\dfrac{(469+174)^2-(469-174)^2}{(469\times174)} = ?$

   (a) 2   (b) 4
   (c) 295   (d) 643

3. A man has some hens and cows. If the number of heads be 48 and the number of feet equals 140, then the number of hens will be:
   (a) 22   (b) 23
   (c) 24   (d) 26

4. Free notebooks were distributed equally among children of a class. The number of notebooks each child got was one-eighth of the number of children. Had the number of children been half, each child would have got 16 notebooks. Total how many notebooks were distributed?
   (a) 256   (b) 432
   (c) 512   (d) 640

5. In a regular week, there are 5 working days and for each day, the working hours are 8. A man gets ₹ 2.40 per hour for regular work and ₹ 3.20 per hours for overtime. If he earns ₹ 432 in 4 weeks, then how many hours does he work for?
   (a) 160   (b) 175
   (c) 180   (d) 195

6. To fill a tank, 25 buckets of water are required. How many buckets of water will be required to fill the same tank if the capacity of the bucket is reduced to two-fifth of its present?
   (a) 10
   (b) 35

   (c) 62.5
   (d) Cannot be determined

7. Eight people are planning to share equally the cost of a rental car. If one person withdraws from the arrangement and the others share equally the entire cost of the car, then the share of each of the remaining persons is increased by:
   (a) 1/7   (b) 1/8
   (c) 1/9   (d) 7/8

8. A fires 5 shots to B's 3 but A kills only once in 3 shots while B kills once in 2 shots. When B has missed 27 times, A has killed:
   (a) 30 birds   (b) 60 birds
   (c) 72 birds   (d) 90 birds

9. One-third of Rahul's savings in National Savings Certificate is equal to one-half of his savings in Public Provident Fund. If he has ₹ 1, 50,000 as total savings, how much has he saved in Public Provident Fund?
   (a) ₹ 30,000   (b) ₹ 50,000
   (c) ₹ 60,000   (d) ₹ 90,000

10. A sum of ₹ 1360 has been divided among A, B and C such that A gets 2/3 of what B gets and B gets 1/4 of what C gets. B's share is:
    (a) ₹ 120   (b) ₹ 160
    (c) ₹ 240   (d) ₹ 300

11. A man has ₹ 480 in the denominations of one-rupee notes, five-rupee notes and ten-rupee notes. The number of notes of each denomination is equal. What is the total number of notes that he has?
    (a) 45   (b) 60
    (c) 75   (d) 90

12. There are two examinations rooms A and B. If 10 students are sent from A to B, then the number of students in each room is the same. If 20 candidates are sent from B to A, then the number of students in A is double the number of students in B. The number of students in room A is:
    (a) 20   (b) 80
    (c) 100   (d) 200

13. The price of 10 chairs is equal to that of 4 tables. The price of 15 chairs and 2 tables together is ₹ 4000. The total price of 12 chairs and 3 tables is:
    (a) ₹ 3500   (b) ₹ 3750
    (c) ₹ 3840   (d) ₹ 3900

14. If $a - b = 3$ and $a^2 + b^2 = 29$, find the value of ab.
    (a) 10   (b) 12
    (c) 15   (d) 18

15. The price of 2 saris and 4 shirts is ₹ 1600. With the same money one can buy 1 sari and 6 shirts. If one wants to buy 12 shirts, how much shall he have to pay?
    (a) ₹ 1200
    (b) ₹ 2400
    (c) ₹ 4800
    (d) Cannot be determined

Answer Key

1. (c)	2. (b)	3. (d)	4. (c)	5. (b)	6. (c)	7. (a)	8. (a)
9. (c)	10. (c)	11. (d)	12. (c)	13. (d)	14. (a)	15. (b)	

Hints and Solutions

1. **(c)**
   Suppose their paths cross after x minutes.
   Then, $11 + 57x = 51 - 63x$
   $\Rightarrow \qquad 120x = 40$
   $\Rightarrow \qquad x = 1/3$
   Number of floors covered by David in (1/3) min. $= 1/3 \times 57 = 19$.
   So, their paths cross at $(11 + 19)$ i.e., 30th floor.

2. **(b)**
   Let $a = 469$
   $b = 469$ there
   given expression $= \dfrac{(a+b)^2 - (a-b)^2}{ab}$
   $\qquad\qquad = 4ab/ab$
   $\qquad\qquad = 4$

3. **(d)**
   Let the number of hens be x and the number of cows be y.
   Then, $x + y = 48$ .... (i)   and $2x + 4y = 140$
   $\Rightarrow \quad x + 2y = 70$ .... (ii)
   Solving (i) and (ii) we get: $x = 26$, $y = 22$.
   $\therefore$ The required answer $= 26$.

4. **(c)**
   Let total number of children be x.
   Then, $x \times (1/8) x = x/2 \times 16 \Leftrightarrow x = 64$
   $\therefore$ Number of notebooks $= x^2/8$
   $\qquad\qquad\qquad = 1/8 \times 64 \times 64 = 512$

5. **(b)**
   Suppose the man works overtime for x hours.
   Now, working hours in 4 weeks $= (5 \times 8 \times 4)$
   $\qquad\qquad\qquad\qquad = 160$
   $\therefore 160 \times 2.40 + x \times 3.20 = 432$
   $\Rightarrow 3.20x = 432 - 384 = 48$
   $\Rightarrow \qquad x = 15$
   Hence, total hours of work $= (160 + 15)$
   $\qquad\qquad\qquad = 175$

6. **(c)**
   Let the capacity of 1 bucket $= x$
   Then, the capacity of tank $= 25x$
   New capacity of bucket $= 2x/5$
   $\therefore$ Required number of buckets
   $= 25x / (2x/5) = 125/2 = 62.5$

7. **(a)**
   Original share of 1 person $= 1/8$
   New share of 1 person $= 1/7$
   Increase $= 1/7 - 1/8 = 1/56$
   $\therefore$ Required fraction $= (1/56) / (1/8) = 1/7$

8. **(a)**
   Let the total number of shots be x. Then,
   Shots fired by A $\quad = 5x/8$
   Shots fired by B $\quad = 3x/8$
   Killing shots by A $= 1/3$ of $5x/8 = 5x/24$
   Shots missed by B $= 1/2$ of $3x/8 = 3x/16$
   $\therefore 3x/16 = 27$ or $x = 144$
   Birds killed by A $= 5x/24 = (5x\ 144)/24$
   $\qquad\qquad\qquad = 30$

9. **(c)**
   Let savings in N.S.C and P.P.F. be ₹ x and Rs. $(150000 - x)$ respectively. Then,
   $1/3x = 1/2(150000 - x)$
   $\Rightarrow x/3 + x/2 = 75000$
   $\Rightarrow \qquad 5x/6 = 75000$
   $\Rightarrow \qquad x = (75000 \times 6)/5 = ₹\ 90000$
   $\therefore$ Savings in Public Provident Fund
   $\qquad = ₹\ (150000 - 90000) = ₹\ 60000$

10. **(c)**
    Let C's share $= ₹\ x$
    Then, B's share $= ₹\ x/4$, A's share $= ₹\ 2/3 \times x/4$
    $\qquad\qquad\qquad\qquad\qquad = ₹\ x/6$
    $\Rightarrow \quad 17x/12 = 1360$
    $\Rightarrow x = (1360 \times 12)/17 = ₹\ 960$
    Hence, B's share $= ₹\ 960/4 = ₹\ 240$

11. **(d)**
    Let number of notes of each denomination be x.
    Then $x + 5x + 10x = 480$
    $\Rightarrow 16x = 480$
    $\therefore x = 30$
    Hence, total number of notes $= 3x = 90$

12. **(c)**
    Let the number of students in rooms A and B be x and y respectively.
    Then, $x - 10 = y + 10 \Rightarrow x - y = 20$ .... (i)
    and $x + 20 = 2(y - 20) \Rightarrow x - 2y = -60$ .... (ii)
    Solving (i) and (ii) we get: $x = 100$, $y = 80$.
    $\therefore$ The required answer $= A = 100$.

International Mathematics Olympiad – Class 6

13. **(d)**

Let the cost of a chair and that of a table be ₹ x and ₹ y respectively.

Then, $10x = 4y$ or $y = 5x/2$.

∴ $15x + 2y = 4000$

⇒ $15x + 2 \times 5x/2 = 4000$

⇒ $20x = 4000$

∴ $x = 200$

So, $y = 5/2 \times 200 = 500$

Hence, the cost of 12 chairs and 3 tables

$= 12x + 3y$

$= ₹ (2400 + 1500)$

$= ₹ 3900$

14. **(a)** Here,

$2ab = (a^2 + b^2) - (a - b)^2$

$= 29 - 9 = 20$

⇒ $ab = 10$

15. **(b)**

Let the price of a sari and a shirt be ₹ x and ₹ y respectively.

Then, $2x + 4y = 1600$ .... (i)

and $x + 6y = 1600$ .... (ii)

Dividing equation (i) by 2, we get the below equation.

$x + 2y = 800$ .... (iii)

Now subtract (iii) from (ii)

$4y = 800$

Therefore, $y = 200$.

Now putting the value of y in (iii)

$x + 2 \times 200 = 800$

$x + 400 = 800$

Therefore $x = 400$

Solving (i) and (ii) we get $x = 400, y = 200$

Cost of 12 shirts $= ₹ (12 \times 200) = ₹ 2400$.

7 Problems on Ages

To solve the problems based on ages, candidates require the knowledge of linear equation. The methods involve some basic concepts as well as some more time than it deserves. Sometimes it is easier to solve the problems by taking the given options in account. But this hit and trial method proves costly sometimes, when we reach our solution much later. In this chapter we have tried to cover all types of questions to minimise your difficulties.

Each of these examples is followed by three statements. You have to study the question and all the three statements given to decide whether any information provided in the statement(s) is redundant and can be dispensed with while answering the given question.

Example 1: What will be the ratio between ages of Sam and Albert after 5 years?

    I.   Sam's present age is more than Albert's present age by 4 years.

    II. Albert's present age is 20 years.

    III. The ratio of Albert's present age to Sam's present age is 5 : 6.

    (a) Any two of I, II and III

    (b) II only

    (c) III only

    (d) I or III only

    (e) II or III only

Solution: Option (a) is correct.
Clearly, any two of the given statements will give the answer and in each case, the third is redundant.
∴ Correct answer is (a).

Example 2: What is the difference between the present ages of Ayush and Deepak?

    I.   The ratio between Ayush's present age and his age after 8 years is 4 : 5.

    II. The ratio between the present ages of Ayush and Deepak is 4 : 3.

    III. The ratio between Deepak's present age and his age four years ago is 6 : 5.

    (a) Any two of I, II and III

    (b) I or III only

    (c) Any one of the three

    (d) All I, II and III are required

    (e) Even with all I, II and III, the answer cannot be obtained.

Solution: Option (a) is correct.
Clearly, any two of the given statements will give the answer and in each case, the third is redundant.

1. Present ages of Sameer and Anand are in the ratio of 5 : 4 respectively. Three years hence, the ratio of their ages will become 11 : 9 respectively. What is Anand's present age in years?
    (a) 24 (b) 27
    (c) 40
    (d) Can not be determined

2. A is two years older than B who is twice as old as C. If the total of the ages of A, B and C be 27, then how old is B?
    (a) 7 (b) 8
    (c) 9 (d) 10

3. A father said to his son, "I was as old as you are at the present at the time of your birth". If the father's age is 38 years now, the son's age five years back was:
    (a) 14 years (b) 19 years
    (c) 33 years (d) 38 years

4. The sum of ages of 5 children born at the intervals of 3 years each is 50 years. What is the age of the youngest child?
    (a) 4 years (b) 8 years
    (c) 10 years (d) None of these

5. Father is aged three times more than his son Ronit. After 8 years, he would be two and a half times of Ronit's age. After further 8 years, how many times would he be of Ronit's age?
    (a) 2 times (b) 3 times
    (c) 5 times (d) 4 times

6. The age of father 10 years ago was thrice the age of his son. Ten years hence, father's age will be twice that of his son. The ratio of their present ages is:
    (a) 5 : 2 (b) 7 : 3
    (c) 9 : 2 (d) 13 : 4

7. Q is as much younger than R as he is older than T. If the sum of the ages of R and T is 50 years, what is definitely the difference between R and Q's age?
    (a) 1 year (b) 2 years
    (c) 25 years (d) Data inadequate

8. A person's present age is two-fifth of the age of his mother. After 8 years, he will be one-half of the age of his mother. How old is the mother at present?
    (a) 32 years (b) 36 years
    (c) 40 years (d) 48 years

9. Ayesha's father was 38 years of age when she was born while her mother was 36 years old when her brother four years younger to her was born. What is the difference between the ages of her parents?
    (a) 2 years (b) 4 years
    (c) 6 years (d) 8 years

10. The present ages of three persons are in proportions 4 : 7 : 9. Eight years ago, the sum of their ages was 56. Find their present ages (in years).
    (a) 8, 20, 28 (b) 16, 28, 36
    (c) 20, 35, 45 (d) None of these

11. A man is 24 years older than his son. In two years, his age will be twice the age of his son. The present age of his son is:
    (a) 14 years (b) 18 years
    (c) 20 years (d) 22 years

12. Six years ago, the ratio of the ages of Kunal and Sagar was 6 : 5. Four years hence, the ratio of their ages will be 11 : 10. What is Sagar's age at present?
    (a) 16 years (b) 18 years
    (c) 20 years
    (d) Cannot be determined

13. The sum of the present ages of a father and his son is 60 years. Six years ago, father's age was five times the age of the son. After 6 years, son's age will be:
    (a) 12 years (b) 14 years
    (c) 18 years (d) 20 years

14. At present, the ratio between the ages of Arun and Deepak is 4 : 3. After 6 years, Arun's age will be 26 years. What is the age of Deepak at present?
    (a) 12 years (b) 15 years
    (c) 19.5 years (d) 21 years

15. Sachin is younger than Rahul by 7 years. If their ages are in the respective ratio of 7 : 9, how old is Sachin?
    (a) 16 years   (b) 18 years
    (c) 28 years   (d) 24.5 years

16. The ratio of the father's age to the son's age is 4 : 1. The product of their ages is 196. What will be the ratio of their ages after 5 years?
    (a) 11 : 4   (b) 4 : 11
    (c) 5 : 12   (d) 2 : 3

17. The ratio of Rita's age to the age of her mother is 3 : 11. The difference of their ages is 24 years. What will be the ratio of their ages after 3 years?
    (a) 2 : 3   (b) 1 : 3
    (c) 2 : 5   (d) 5 : 7

18. The sum of ages of a mother and her daughter is 50 years. Also 5 years ago, the mother's age was 7 times the age of the daughter. What are the present ages of the mother and the daughter?
    (a) 40 years , 10 years
    (b) 20 years , 10 years
    (c) 30 years , 15 years
    (d) 40 years , 15 years

19. The sum of the ages of a son and a father is 56 years. After 4 years, the age of the father will be three times that of the son. What is the age of the son?
    (a) 14 years   (b) 16 years
    (c) 12 years   (d) 17 years

20. 10 years ago, Sita's mother was 4 times older than her daughter. After 10 years, the mother will be two times older than the daughter. What is the present age of Sita?
    (a) 20 years   (b) 30 years
    (c) 25 years   (d) 35 years

Answer Key

1. (a)	2. (d)	3. (a)	4. (a)	5. (a)	6. (b)	7. d	8. (c)
9. (c)	10. (b)	11. (d)	12. (a)	13. (d)	14. (b)	15. d	16. (a)
17. (b)	18. (a)	19. (c)	20. (a)				

1. **(a)**
   Let the present ages of Sameer and Anand be $5x$ years and $4x$ years respectively.

   Then, $\dfrac{5x+3}{4x+3}=\dfrac{11}{9}$

   $\Rightarrow 9(5x+3)=11(4x+3)$
   $\Rightarrow 45x+27=44x+33$
   $\Rightarrow 45x-44x=33-27$
   $\Rightarrow x=6$
   $\therefore$ Anand's present age $=4x=4\times 6=24$ years.

2. **(d)**
   Let C's age be x years. Then, B's age $=2x$ years. A's age $=(2x+2)$ years.
   $\therefore (2x+2)+2x+x=27$
   $\Rightarrow 5x=25$
   $\Rightarrow x=5$
   Hence, B's age $=2x=2\times 5=10$ years.

3. **(a)**
   Let the son's present age be x years. Then,
   $(38-x)=x$
   $\Rightarrow 2x=38$
   $\Rightarrow x=19$
   $\therefore$ Son's age 5 years back $=(19-5)$
   $=14$ years

4. **(a)**
   Let the ages of children be x, $(x+3)$, $(x+6)$, $(x+9)$ and $(x+12)$ years.
   Then, $x+(x+3)+(x+6)+(x+9)+(x+12)$
   $=50$
   $\Rightarrow 5x=20$
   $\Rightarrow x=4$
   $\therefore$ Age of the youngest child $=x=4$ years.

5. **(a)**
   Let Ronit's present age be x years. Then, father's present age $=(x+3x)$ years $=4x$ years.
   $\therefore (4x+8)=5/2(x+8)$
   $\Rightarrow 8x+16=5x+40$
   $\Rightarrow 3x=24$
   $\Rightarrow x=8$
   Hence, required ratio $=(4x+16)/(x+16)$
   $=48/24=2$

6. **(b)**
   Let the ages of father and son 10 years ago be $3x$ and x years respectively.
   Then, $(3x+10)+10=2[(x+10)+10]$
   $\Rightarrow 3x+20=2x+40$

   $\Rightarrow x=20$
   $\therefore$ Required ratio $=(3x+10):(x+10)$
   $=70:30=7:3$.

7. **(d)**
   Given that:
   1. The difference of age b/w R and Q = The difference of age b/w Q and T.
   2. Sum of age of R and T is 50 i.e. $(R+T)$
      $=50$

   Question: $R-Q=?$
   Explanation:
   $R-Q=Q-T$
   $\Rightarrow (R+T)=2Q$
   Now given that $(R+T)=50$
   So, $50=2Q$ and therefore $Q=25$
   Question is $(R-Q)=?$
   Here we know the value(age) of Q (25), but we don't know the age of R.
   Therefore, $(R-Q)$ cannot be determined.

8. **(c)**
   Let the mother's present age be x years.
   Then, the person's present age $=2x/5$ years.
   $\therefore (2x/5+8)=1/2(x+8)$
   $\Rightarrow 2(2x+40)=5(x+8)$
   $\Rightarrow x=40$

9. **(c)**
   Mother's age when Ayesha's brother was born $=36$ years.
   Father's age when Ayesha's brother was born $=(38+4)$ years $=42$ years.
   $\therefore$ Required difference $=(42-36)$ years
   $=6$ years

10. **(b)**
    Let their present ages be $4x$, $7x$ and $9x$ years respectively.
    Then, $(4x-8)+(7x-8)+(9x-8)=56$
    $\Rightarrow 20x=80$
    $\Rightarrow x=4$
    $\therefore$ Their present ages are $4x=16$ years, $7x=28$ years and $9x=36$ years respectively.

11. **(d)**
    Let the son's present age be x years. Then, man's present age $=(x+24)$ years.
    $\therefore (x+24)+2=2(x+2)$
    $\Rightarrow x+26=2x+4$
    $\Rightarrow x=22$

12. **(a)**

Let the ages of Kunal and Sagar 6 years ago be $6x$ and $5x$ years respectively.

Then, $(6x + 6) + 4 = 11$
$(5x + 6) + 4 = 10$
$\Rightarrow 10(6x + 10) = 11(5x + 10)$
$\Rightarrow 5x = 10$
$\Rightarrow x = 2$
∴ Sagar's present age = $(5x + 6) = 16$ years.

13. **(d)**

Let the present ages of son and father be x and $(60 - x)$ years respectively.

Then, $(60 - x) - 6 = 5(x - 6)$
$\Rightarrow 54 - x = 5x - 30$
$\Rightarrow 6x = 84$
$\Rightarrow x = 14$
∴ Son's age after 6 years = $(x + 6) = 20$ years.

14. **(b)**

Let the present ages of Arun and Deepak be $4x$ years and $3x$ years respectively. Then,
$4x + 6 = 26 \iff 4x = 20$
$\Rightarrow x = 5$
∴ Deepak's age = $3x = 15$ years.

15. **(d)**

Let Rahul's age be x years.
Then, Sachin's age = $(x - 7)$ years.
∴ $(x - 7) / x = 7/9$
$\Rightarrow 9x - 63 = 7x$
$\Rightarrow 2x = 63$
$\Rightarrow x = 31.5$
Hence, Sachin's age = $(x - 7) = 24.5$ years.

16. **(a)**

Let the ratio of their proportionality be x.
Then,
$4x \times x = 196$

$\Rightarrow 4x^2 = 196$
$\Rightarrow x = 7$
Thus, father's age = 28 years and son's age
= 7 years
After 5 years, father's age = 33 years and son's age = 12 years
∴ Ratio = 33 : 12 = 11 : 4

17. **(b)**

Difference in ratios = 8
Then $8 \equiv 24 \qquad \therefore 1 \equiv 3$
Thus, value of 1 in ratio is equivalent to 3 years.
Thus, Rita's age = $3 \times 3 = 9$ years
Mother's age = $11 \times 3 = 33$ years
After 3 years, the ratio = 12 : 36 = 1 : 3

18. **(a)**

Let the age of the daughter be x years.
Then, the age of the mother is $(50 - x)$ years
5 years ago, $7(x - 5) = 50 - x - 5$
or, $8x = 50 - 5 + 35 = 80$
∴ $x = 10$
Therefore, daughter's age = 10 years and mother's age = 40 years.

19. **(c)**

Let the age of the son be x years.
Then, the age of the father is $(56 - x)$ years
After 4 years, $3(x + 4) = 56 - x + 4$
or, $4x = 56 + 4 - 12 = 48$
∴ $x = 12$ years
Thus, son's age = 12 years

20. **(a)**

Daughter's age
$= \dfrac{10(4-1) + 10(2-1)}{4-2} = 20 \text{ years}$

8   Ratio and Proportion

Ratio

The ratio of two numbers x and y is the fraction $\dfrac{x}{y}$ and it can be written as $x : y$.

To find the ratio of two like quantities they should be changed into the same unit of measurement.

Example 1:   What is the ratio of 15 seconds to 1 hour.

Solution: $\dfrac{15\,\text{seconds}}{1\,\text{hour}} = \dfrac{15\,\text{seconds}}{60 \times 60\,\text{seconds}}$

$\qquad\qquad\qquad = \dfrac{1}{240} = 1 : 240$

Example 2:   What is the equivalent ratio of 5 : 6?

Solution: Here, $5 : 6 = \dfrac{5}{6} = \dfrac{5 \times 2}{6 \times 2} = \dfrac{10}{12} = 10 : 12$

Example 3:   Two numbers are in the ratio 5 : 4. If their sum is 324. Find the numbers.

Solution: If numbers are $5x$ and $4x$, then $5x + 4x = 324$

$\Rightarrow \qquad 9x = 324$

$\Rightarrow \qquad x = \dfrac{324}{9} = 36$

$\Rightarrow \qquad 5x = 5 \times 36 = 180$

and $\qquad 4x = 4 \times 36 = 144$

Example 4:   A 35 cm line segment is divided into two parts in the ratio 3 : 4. Find the smaller part.

Solution: Here, $3x + 4x = 35$

$\Rightarrow 7x = 35 \Rightarrow x = \dfrac{35}{7} = 5$

$\therefore$ Smaller part $= 3x = 3 \times 5 = 15$ cm

Proportion

If two ratios are equal then they are said to be in proportion.

It is denoted by : : or =.

If $\, p : q :: r : s$ then

and p & s are called extremes

q & r are called means.

Here, Product of extremes = product of means.

Example 5:   If $36 : 81 :: x : 63$ then find the value of x.

Solution: Given $36 : 81 :: x : 63$

$\Rightarrow 36 \times 63 = 81 \times x$

$\Rightarrow \qquad x = \dfrac{36 \times 63}{81} = 28$

Example 6: Find the missing proportion of $3.5 : 3 :: x : 6$

Solution: Here, $3.5 : 3 :: x : 6$

$\Rightarrow 3 \times x = 3.5 \times 6$

$\Rightarrow \quad x = \dfrac{3.5 \times 6}{3} = 7$

Example 7: The first, second and third terms of a proportion are 12, 21 and 8 respectively what is the fourth term?

Solution: If x is fourth term then $12 : 21 :: 8 : x$

$\Rightarrow 12 \times x = 21 \times 8$

$\Rightarrow \quad x = \dfrac{21 \times 8}{12} = 14$

Unitary Method

In this method, first we find the value of a unit of the item from the given information and then we calculate the desired value from the unit value. In this method to get more we multiply and to get less we divide.

Example 8: Mohan's salary of 9 months is ₹ 21000 what is the salary of 15 months?

Solution: Mohan's salary of 9 months = 21000

Mohan's salary of 1 month = $\dfrac{21000}{9}$

$\therefore$ Mohan's salary of 15 months = $\dfrac{21000 \times 15}{9}$ = ₹ 35000

Example 9: The cost of a dozen apple is ₹ 168. What is the cost of 25 apples?

Solution:

The cost of 12 apple = ₹ 168

The cost of 1 apple = ₹ $\dfrac{168}{12}$

The cost of 25 apple = ₹ $\dfrac{168 \times 25}{12}$

$= 14 \times 25 = $ Rs. 350

Example 10: If a bus covers a distance of 75 km in one hour. Find the distance covered by the bus in 45 minutes.

Solution:

In 60 minutes the bus covers 75 km.

$\therefore$ In 1 minute the bus covers $= \dfrac{75}{60}$ km

In 45 minutes the bus covers $= \dfrac{75 \times 45}{60}$

$= 56.25$ km

1. 12 boys can dig a pitch in 12 hours. How long will 18 boys take to do it ?
   (a) 8 hours   (b) 6 hours
   (c) 9 hours   (d) 12 hours

2. If a bus covers 225 km in 3 hours and a train covers 600 km in 5 hours. What is the ratio of their speeds?
   (a) 5 : 8   (b) 3 : 5
   (c) 5 : 7   (d) 3 : 8

3. The angles of a triangle are in the ratio 2 : 3 : 5. What is the measure of the largest angle?
   (a) 70°   (b) 80°
   (c) 90°   (d) 100°

4. If 36 men can finish a piece of work in 36 days. How many men will be required to finish it in 24 days?
   (a) 36   (b) 52
   (c) 54   (d) 56

5. If x, y, z are in proportion then which of the following is true?
   (a) $y^2 = xz$ (b) $x^2 = yz$
   (c) $z^2 = xy$ (d) None of these

6. If 35 envelop costs ` 87.50 how many such envelops can we purchase for ` 315?
   (a) 116   (b) 126
   (c) 216   (d) 136

7. The weight of 65 magzines is 13 kg. What is the weight of 80 such magazines?
   (a) 14kg   (b) 16kg
   (c) 15kg   (d) 17kg

8. The boys and girls in a school are in the ratio 9 : 5. If the total strength of the school is 994. What is the number of girls?
   (a) 355   (b) 365
   (c) 375   (d) 385

9. The ratio of length of a field to its width is 5 : 3. What is the length if the width is 36 cm?
   (a) 60cm   (b) 48cm
   (c) 72cm   (d) 84cm

10. If ₹ 1020 is divided among A, B, C in the ratio 2 : 3 : 5. What is the share of C?
    (a) ₹ 410   (b) ₹ 510
    (c) ₹ 408   (d) ₹ 612

11. If ₹ 8100 is divided among L, M, N in the ratio 2 : 3 : 4. What amount does M receive?
    (a) ₹ 4500   (b) ₹ 3600
    (c) ₹ 1800   (d) ₹ 2700

12. A bus travels 183 km in 3 hours and a train travels 426 km in 6 hours. What is the ratio of their speeds?
    (a) 51 : 71   (b) 61 : 71
    (c) 61 : 73   (d) None of these

13. Mohan's salary of 9 months is ₹ 21000. What is his salary of 15 months?
    (a) ₹ 32000   (b) ₹ 33000
    (c) ₹ 35000   (d) None of these

14. If one dozen bananas cost ₹ 36. What is the cost of 26 bananas?
    (a) ₹ 72   (b) ₹ 78
    (c) ₹ 74   (d) ₹ 76

15. The cost of 2 kg of apples is ₹ 120. How many kilograms of apples can be purchased for Rs. 720 ?
    (a) 8 kg   (b) 10 kg
    (c) 12 kg   (d) 14 kg

16. Weight of 8 containers containing milk is 72 kg. What is the weight of 18 such containers?
    (a) 152 kg   (b) 162 kg
    (c) 142 kg   (d) 172 kg

17. The cost of two dozen oranges is ₹ 168. What will be the cost of 16 oranges?
    (a) ₹ 96   (b) ₹ 124
    (c) ₹ 102   (d) ₹ 112

18. Find the 1st term if 2nd, 3rd & 4th terms of a proportion are 12, 14 and 8 respectively.
    (a) 21   (b) 24
    (c) 18   (d) 28

19. What is the ratio of 40 cm to 1.5 m?
    (a) 4 : 15   (b) 2 : 15
    (c) 3 : 5   (d) 5 : 3

20. What is the value of x if
    $x : 92 : : 87 : 116$?
    (a) 76   (b) 69
    (c) 96   (d) 78

21. If 9, x, x 49 are in proportion then what is the value of x?
    (a) 21   (b) 23
    (c) 26   (d) 31

22. If 25, 35, x are in proportion then the value of x is
    (a) 35   (b) 49
    (c) 56   (d) 63

23. In a proportion 1st, 2nd and 4th terms are 7, 42 and 72 respectively. What is the third term?
    (a) 8   (b) 12
    (c) 14   (d) 16

24. Ranjit earns ₹ 15300 and saves ₹ 1224 per month. What is the ratio of his income and expenditure?
    (a) 25 : 23   (b) 27 : 25
    (c) 29 : 25   (d) 31 : 29

25. Mahesh earns ₹ 16400 and his expenditure is ₹ 7400. What is the ratio of his saving and earning?
    (a) 41 : 83   (b) 45 : 82
    (c) 47 : 81   (d) 49 : 82

26. The ratio of income to expenditure of a man is 7 : 6. What is the saving if the income is ₹ 28000?
    (a) ₹ 9600   (b) ₹ 8000
    (c) ₹ 6000   (d) ₹ 4000

27. What is the ratio of 15 minutes to 2 hours?
    (a) 1 : 4   (b) 1 : 6
    (c) 1 : 8   (d) 1 : 10

28. What is the ratio of 210 grams to 7kg?
    (a) 3 : 10   (b) 3 : 100
    (c) 3 : 1000   (d) None of these

29. What is the ratio of 1.2km to 300m?
    (a) 8 : 1   (b) 5 : 1
    (c) 4 : 1   (d) 6 : 1

30. If $36 : x : : x : 16$, what is the value of x.
    (a) 18   (b) 24
    (c) 16   (d) 32

Answer Key

1. (a)	2. (a)	3. (c)	4. (c)	5. (a)	6. (b)	7. (b)	8. (c)	9. (a)	10. (b)
11. (d)	12. (b)	13. (c)	14. (b)	15. (c)	16. (b)	17. (d)	18. (a)	19. (a)	20. (b)
21. (a)	22. (b)	23. (b)	24. (a)	25. (b)	26. (d)	27. (c)	28. (b)	29. (c)	30. (b)

1. **(a)**

   12 boys can dig a pitch in 12 hours

   ∴ 1 boy can dig a pitch in 12 × 12 hours

   Hence, 18 boys can dig a pitch in $\dfrac{12 \times 12}{18}$

   $= 8$ hours

2. **(a)**

   $\dfrac{\text{speed of bus}}{\text{speed of train}} = \dfrac{225 \div 3}{600 \div 5} = \dfrac{75}{120} = \dfrac{5}{8}$

3. **(c)** Here,

   $2x + 3x + 5x = 180$

   $\Rightarrow 10x = 180$

   $\Rightarrow x = \dfrac{180}{10} = 18$

   ∴ Largest angle $= 5x = 5 \times 18 = 90°$

4. **(c)**

   In 36 days the work is finished by 36 men

   In 1 day the work is finished 36 × 36

   On 24 days the work is finished $= \dfrac{36 \times 36}{24}$

   $= 54$ men

5. **(a)** If x, y, z are in proportion then

   $\dfrac{x}{y} = \dfrac{y}{z} \Rightarrow y^2 = xz$

6. **(b)**

   No. of envelops $= \dfrac{35}{87.50} \times 315$

   $= \dfrac{350 \times 315}{875} = 126$

7. **(b)**

   Weight of 65 magazines $= 13$ kg

   ∴ Weight of 1 magazine $= \dfrac{13}{65}$ kg

   Weight of 80 magazines $= \dfrac{13}{65} \times 80 = 16$ kg

8. **(c)** Given,

   $\dfrac{\text{boys}}{\text{girls}} = \dfrac{9}{5}$

   ∴ No. of girls $= \dfrac{5}{9+5} \times 994$

   $= \dfrac{5}{14} \times 994 = 5 \times 71$

   $= 375$

9. **(a)** Given,

   $\dfrac{\text{length}}{\text{width}} = \dfrac{5}{3} = \dfrac{L}{36}$

   $L = \dfrac{5 \times 36}{3} = 60$ cm

10. **(b)** Given,

    $2x + 3x + 5x = 1020$

    $\Rightarrow \qquad 10x = 1020$

    $\Rightarrow \qquad x = \dfrac{1020}{10} = 102$

    ∴ Share of C $= 5 \times 102 = 510$

11. **(d)**

    Amount of M $= \dfrac{3}{2+3+4} \times 8100$

    $= \dfrac{3}{9} \times 8100$

    $= 3 \times 900$

    $= ₹ 2700$

12. **(b)**

    $\dfrac{\text{speed of bus}}{\text{speed of train}} = \dfrac{183 \div 3}{426 \div 6} = \dfrac{61}{71}$

13. **(c)**

    Salary of 15 months $= \dfrac{21000 \times 15}{9}$

    $= ₹ 35000$

14. **(b)**

    Cost of 26 bananas $= \dfrac{36 \times 26}{12} = ₹ 78$

15. **(c)**

Required weight $= \dfrac{2}{120} \times 720 = 12\,\text{kg}$

16. **(b)**

Required weight $= \dfrac{72}{8} \times 18 = 162$ kg

17. **(d)**

Cost of 16 oranges $= \dfrac{168}{24} \times 16 = ₹\ 112$

18. **(a)** If x is first term, then

$x : 12 :: 14 : 8$

$\Rightarrow \dfrac{x}{12} = \dfrac{14}{8} \Rightarrow x = \dfrac{14 \times 12}{8} = 21$

19. **(a)**

$\dfrac{40\ \text{cm}}{1.5\ \text{m}} = \dfrac{40\ \text{cm}}{150\ \text{cm}} = \dfrac{4}{15} = 4 : 15$

20. **(b)** Given,

$x : 92 :: 87 : 116$

$\Rightarrow \dfrac{x}{92} = \dfrac{87}{116}$

$\Rightarrow \quad x = \dfrac{92 \times 87}{116} = 69$

21. **(a)** Given,

$9 : x :: x : 49$

$\Rightarrow \dfrac{9}{x} = \dfrac{x}{49} \Rightarrow x \times x = 9 \times 49$

$\Rightarrow x^2 = 9 \times 49$

$\Rightarrow x = \sqrt{9 \times 49} = 3 \times 7 = 21$

22. **(b)** Given,

$25 : 35 :: 35 : x$

$\Rightarrow \dfrac{25}{35} = \dfrac{35}{x} \Rightarrow x = \dfrac{35 \times 35}{25} = 49$

23. **(b)** Given,

$7 : 42 :: x : 72$

$\Rightarrow \dfrac{7}{42} = \dfrac{x}{72} \Rightarrow x = \dfrac{7 \times 72}{42} = 12$

24. **(a)** Given,

Income $= ₹\ 15300$

Saving $= ₹\ 1224$

Here, Expenditure $= 15300 - 1224 = 14076$.

$\dfrac{\text{Income}}{\text{Expenditure}} = \dfrac{15300}{14076} = \dfrac{25}{23} = 25 : 23$

25. **(b)**

Earning $= ₹\ 16400$

Expenditure $= ₹\ 7400$

Saving $= 16400 - 7400 = 9000$

$\dfrac{\text{Saving}}{\text{Earning}} = \dfrac{9000}{16400} = \dfrac{90}{164} = \dfrac{45}{82} = 45 : 82$

26. **(d)** Given,

$\dfrac{\text{Saving}}{\text{Income}} = \dfrac{1}{7} \Rightarrow \dfrac{x}{28000} = \dfrac{1}{7}$

$x = \dfrac{28000}{7} = 4000$

27. **(c)** Here,

$\dfrac{15\ \text{minutes}}{2\ \text{hours}} = \dfrac{15}{2 \times 60} = \dfrac{1}{8} = 1 : 8$

28. **(b)** Here,

$\dfrac{210\ \text{grams}}{7\ \text{kg}} = \dfrac{210}{7 \times 1000} = \dfrac{3}{100} = 3 : 100$

29. **(c)** Here,

$\dfrac{1.2\ \text{km}}{300\ \text{m}} = \dfrac{1.2 \times 1000}{300} = \dfrac{12}{3} = 4 : 1$

30. **(b)** Given

$\dfrac{36}{}_{16} \Rightarrow x^2 = 36 \times 16$

$x = \sqrt{36 \times 16} = 6 \times 4 = 24$

It is generalized arithmetic in which numbers are represented by letters called literals.

Addition

The sum of a literal x and a number $5 = x + 5$ P more than $n = n + p$

Subtraction

5 less than a literal $P = P - 5$

$$m \text{ less than } x = x - m$$

Multiplication

7 times x is written as $7x$. The product of a and $b = ab$.

For any literals x, y, z

$$x \times 1 = 1 \times x = x$$
$$x \times y = y \times x$$
$$(x\,y)\,z = x\,(y\,z)$$
$$x\,(y + z) = xy + xz.$$

Division

x divided by z is written as $\dfrac{x}{z}$.

x divided by 4 is $\dfrac{x}{4}$

17 divided by t is $\dfrac{17}{t}$.

Example 1: Write the following using numbers, literal, and basic signs.

(a) 17 taken away from the sum of a & b.

(b) One – fifth of sum of $P + d$.

Solution: (a) $a + b - 17$

(b) $\dfrac{p+d}{5}$

Example 2: Write the following in the exponential form

(a) $7 \times x \times x \times x \times y \times y \times z \times z \times z$

(b) $b \times b \times b \times b$ .... 7 times

Solution:

(a) $7x^3 y^2 z^3$

(b) b^7

Constant

A symbol having a fixed numerical value is called constant.

Example: 2, –4, 6, etc.

Variable

A symbol having various numerical values is called a variable.

Area of rectangle = a × b, Here, a and b are variables.

Algebraic Expression

It is a combination of constants and variables connected by any one or more of the basic operations.

Example: $3x + 5y - 2xyz$

Types of Algebraic Expressions

(1) **Monomial:** An expression which contains only one term is known as a monomial.
Example: $5x$, $2xy^2$, $-7abc$

(2) **Binomial:** An expression containing two terms is called a binomial.
Example: $x + y$, $x - y$ etc.

(3) **Trinomial:** An expression containing three terms is called a trinomial.
Example: $a + b - c$, $x^2 - y^2 + z^2$ etc

Polynomial

An expression containing two or more terms is called a polynomial.

Example: $a^2 - ab + b^2$, $a^2 - bc + b^2 - abc$ etc.

Factor

When two or more numbers and literal are multiplied then each one of them is called a factor of the product

Example: In $7xy^2$, 7 is a numerical factor and x and y^2 are literal factors.

Coefficient

In a product of numbers and literals any of the factors is called the co-efficient of the product of other factors.

Example: In $7xy$, the co-efficient of x is $7y$ and co–efficient of y is $7x$.

Constant Term

A term of the expression which has no literal factor is known an constant term.

Example: In $x^2 + xy - 7$, the constant term $= -7$

Like Terms

The terms having the same literal factors are called like terms.

Example: In the expression $3x^2y - 2xy^2 - 4xy - 8yx^2$, $3x^2y$ & $-8y\,x^2$ are like terms.

Unlike Terms

The terms not having the same literal factors are called unlike terms.

Example: In expression $3x^2 - 5xy + 7y^2$, $3x^2$, $-5xy$, $7y^2$ are unlike terms.

Substitution

The process of replacing the literals by their numerical value is called substitution

Example 3: If $x = 2$, $y = -1$ and $z = 5$, find the value of $x^3 + y^3 + z^3 - 3xyz$.

Solution: $x^3 + y^3 + z^3 - 3xyz$
$= (2)^3 + (-1)^3 + (5)^3 - 3(2)(-1)(5)$
$= 8 - 1 + 125 + 30 = 163 - 1 = 162.$

Example 4: Write down the co-efficient of $x^2\,yz$ in $-3x^2m\,yz$

Solution: Co–efficient of $x^2\,yz = -3m$.

Example 5: Make the like terms in the following $x^2, 2xy, y^2, x^3, -4x^2, 7nx^2$.

Solution: $x^2, -4x^2, 7mx^2$ are like terms.

Rule of Addition

The sum of several like terms with another like terms whose co–efficient is the sum of the co–efficient of the like terms.

Example 6: Add the following

$2x^3 - 3x^2 - 5x + 3,\ 5x^3 + 4x^2 - x - 8$ and $7 + 4x + x^2 - 4x^3$.

Solution: $(2x^3 + 5x^3 - 4x^3) + (-3x^2 + 4x^2 + x^2) + (-5x - x + 4x) + (3 - 8 + 7)$

$= 3x^3 + 2x^2 - 2x + 2$

Example 7: Subtract $6x^3 - 7x^2 + 5x - 3$ from $3 - x + 4x^2 - 7x^3$.

Solution: $(3 - x + 4x^2 - 7x^3) - (6x^3 - 7x^2 + 5x - 3)$

$= 3 - x + 4x^2 - 7x^3 - 6x^3 + 7x^2 - 5x + 3$

$= 6 - 6x + 11x^2 - 13x^3$.

Example 8: Simplify

$2m - 3n - [3m - 2n - \{m - p - m + 2n\}]$

Solution: $= 2m - 3n - [3m - 2n - \{m - p - m + 2n\}]$

$= 2m - 3n - [\,3m - 2n + p - 2n]$

$= 2m - 3n - 3m + 4n - p$

$= -m + n - p.$

$= n - m - p.$

Linear Equation

An equation in which the highest power of the variable involved is 1 is called a linear equation.

Example 9: Write following statement as an equation.

(a) 5 subtracted from thrice a number is 20.

(b) 3 less than 4 times a number is 17.

Solution: (a) $3x - 5 = 20$

(b) $4x - 3 = 17$

Example 10: Solve $3(x + 3) - 2(x - 1) = 5(x - 5)$

Solution: Here, given equation

$3x + 9 - 2x + 2 = 5x - 25$

or, $x + 11 = 5x - 25$

or, $5x - x = 11 + 25$

or, $4x = 36$

$x = \dfrac{36}{4} = 9$

Example 11: Dinesh is twice as old as his brother Mukesh. If the difference of their ages is 11 years find their present ages.

Solution: Let Mukesh's age be x then Dinesh's age $= 2x$.

$\therefore 2x - x = 11 \Rightarrow x = 11$

Their ages are 11 years and 22 years.

1. What must be subtracted from $a^3 - 4a^2 + 5a - 6$ to obtain $a^2 - 2a + 1$?
   (a) $a^3 - 5a^2 + 7a - 7$
   (b) $a^3 - 4a^2 + 7a - 6$
   (c) $a^3 - 5a^3 + 5a - 7$
   (d) None of these

2. By how much does 1 exceed $2x - 3y - 4$?
   (a) $3y - 2x + 3$ (b) $3y + 2x + 3$
   (c) $2x - 3y - 5$ (d) $3y - 2x + 5$

3. How much less than $l - 2m + 3n$ is $2l - 4m - n$?
   (a) $l - 2m - 4n$ (b) $-l + 2m + 4n$
   (c) $-l + 2m - 4n$ (d) $l - 2m + 4n$

4. If $x = -2$ $y = -1$ and $z = 3$ then what is the value of $x^2 + y^2 - z^2$
   (a) -2 (b) -4
   (c) -8 (d) -12

5. What is the co-efficient of m in $-7\,12\,mn$?
   (a) -7 (b) -712
   (c) $-712\,n$ (d) None of these

6. If $x = 4$, $y = -1$ and $z = -2$ then what is the value of $2x^2 - y^2 + 3z^2$?
   (a) 42 (b) 43
   (c) 41 (d) 45

7. What must be added to $5x^3 - 2x^2 + 6x + 7$ to make the sum $x^3 + 3x^2 - x + 1$?
   (a) $-4x^3 + 3x^2 - 6x - 7$
   (b) $-4x^3 + 5x^2 - 7x - 6$
   (c) $4x^3 + 3x^2 - 7x - 6$
   (d) None of these

8. By how much is $2x - 3y + 4z$ greater than $2x + 5y - 6z + 2$?
   (a) $8y - 10z + 2$ (b) $-8y + 10z - 2$
   (c) $8y - 10z - 2$ (d) $-8y + 10z + 2$

9. What is the simplified value of $2x - [3y - \{2x - (y - x)\}]$?
   (a) $4x - 5y$ (b) $5x - 4y$
   (c) $5x - 6y$ (d) $5x - 3y$

10. What is the value of m if
    $$\frac{2m}{3} + 8 = \frac{m}{2} - 1?$$
    (a) 54 (b) -54
    (c) 52 (d) -52

11. What is the value of x?
    $$3(x + 6) + 2(x + 3) = 64$$
    (a) 8 (b) 6
    (c) -8 (d) 4

12. What is the value of P if
    $$3(2 - 5P) - 2(1 - 6P) = 1?$$
    (a) -2 (b) -1
    (c) 2 (d) 1

13. If 8 is subtracted from three times a number the result is 13. What is number?
    (a) 7 (b) 5
    (c) 8 (d) 9

14. The sum of three consecutive natural numbers is 114. Which is the greatest number?
    (a) 37 (b) 38
    (c) 39 (d) 41

15. The length of a rectangular field is 5m more than its breadth. If the perimeter of the field is 74 m what is its length?
    (a) 16m   (b) 17m
    (c) 21m   (d) 23m

16. If 9 is added to a certain number, the result is 57, what is that number?
    (a) 38 (b) 24
    (c) 46 (d) 84

17. If 7 is subtracted from a number, we get 37, then what is that number?
    (a) 42 (b) 44
    (c) 46 (d) 43

18. A man is thrice as old as his daughter. 5 years ago the man was four times as old as his daughter, what is the age of the daughter?
    (a) 10 years   (b) 12 years
    (c) 14 years   (d) 15 years

19. Karan's father is thrice as old as Karan. After 14 years his age will be twice that of his son. What is the age of Karan?
    (a) 12 years
    (b) 14 years
    (c) 15 years
    (d) 16 years

20. The sum of three consecutive even numbers is 78. Which number is smallest among them?
    (a) 24
    (b) 26
    (c) 28
    (d) None of these

21. Five times the price of a radio is ₹ 170 more than three times its price. What is the price of the radio?
    (a) ₹ 85
    (b) ₹ 95
    (c) ₹ 105
    (d) None of these

22. The length of a rectangular park is thrice its breadth. If the perimeter of the park is 168m, what is its breadth?
    (a) 17 m
    (b) 21m
    (c) 19m
    (d) 23m

23. Kiran multiplies a certain number by 17 and adds 4 to the product, she gets 225. What is that number?
    (a) 19
    (b) 15
    (c) 13
    (d) 17

24. What is the sum of the expressions $3a - 2b + 5c$, $2a + 5b - 7c$ and $-a - b + c$?
    (a) $4a - 2b + 2c$
    (b) $4a + 2b - 2c$
    (c) $4a - 2b - c$
    (d) $4a + 2b - c$

25. What is the co-efficient of x^3 in $4y^2zx^3$?
    (a) 4
    (b) $4y^2$
    (c) $4y^2z$
    (d) None of these

26. What is the value of
    $2a - [3b - \{a - (2c - 3b) + 4c - 3(a - b - 2c)\}]$
    (a) $2b + 6c$
    (b) $3b + 8c$
    (c) $4b + 5c$
    (d) $3b + 7c$

27. What is the value of
    $xy - [yz - zx - \{yx - (3y - xz) - (xy - zy)\}]$?
    (a) $xy - xz - 3y$
    (b) $xy + 2xz - 3y$
    (c) $xy - xz + 3y$
    (d) None of these

28. What is the value of x?
    $$\frac{x}{8} - \frac{1}{2} = \frac{x}{6} - 2$$
    (a) 28
    (b) 32
    (c) 34
    (d) 36

29. If a number is tripled and the result is increased by 7, we get 70, then what is the number?
    (a) 21
    (b) 23
    (c) 24
    (d) 27

30. A wire of length 86cm is bent in the form of a rectangle such that its length is 7 cm more than its breadth. What is its length ?
    (a) 21 cm
    (b) 23 cm
    (c) 25 cm
    (d) 27 cm

Answer Key

1. (a)	2. (d)	3. (b)	4. (b)	5. (c)	6. (b)	7. (b)	8. (d)	9. (b)	10 (b)
11. (a)	12. (d)	13. (a)	14. (c)	15. (c)	16. (b)	17. (a)	18. (d)	19. (b)	20. (a)
21. (a)	22. (b)	23. (c)	24. (d)	25. (c)	26. (b)	27. (b)	28. (d)	29. (a)	30. (c)

Hints and Solutions

1. **(a)** Here, $a^3 - 4a^2 + 5a - 6 - (a^2 - 2a + 1)$
$= a^3 - 4a^2 + 5a - 6 - a^2 + 2a - 1$
$= a^3 - 5a^2 + 7a - 7$

2. **(d)** Required difference $= 1 - (2x - 3y - 4)$
$= 3y - 2x + 5$

3. **(b)** Required difference
$= (l - 2m + 3n) - (2l - 4m - n)$
$= -l + 2m + 4n$

4. **(b)** Required value
$= x^2 + y^2 - z^2$
$= (-2)^2 + (-1)^2 - (3)^2 = 4 + 1 - 9$
$= 5 - 9 = -4$

5. **(c)**

6. **(b)** $2x^2 - y^2 + 3z^2$
$= 2(4)^2 - (-1)^2 + 3(-2)^2$
$= 32 - 1 + 12 = 44 - 1 = 43$

7. **(b)** $x^3 + 3x^2 - x + 1 - 5x^3 + 2x^2 - 6x - 7$
$= -4x^3 + 5x^2 - 7x - 6$

8. **(d)** Required difference
$= -(-2x - 5y + 6z - 2)$
$= -8y + 10z + 2$

9. **(b)** $2x - [3y - \{2x - (y-x)\}]$
$= 2x - [3y - \{2x - y + x)\}]$
$= 2x - [3y - 3x + y] = 2x - 4y + 3x = 5x - 4y$

10. **(b)** Given $\dfrac{2m}{3} + 8 = \dfrac{m}{2} - 1$
$\Rightarrow \dfrac{m}{2} - \dfrac{2m}{3} = 8 + 1$.
$\Rightarrow -\dfrac{3m - 4m}{6} = 9$
$\Rightarrow -m = 6 \times 9 \Rightarrow m = -54$

11. **(a)** $3(x + 6) + 2(x + 3) = 64$
$\Rightarrow 3x + 18 + 2x + 6 = 64$
$\Rightarrow 5x + 24 = 64$
$\Rightarrow 5x = 64 - 24$
$\Rightarrow 5x = 40$
$\Rightarrow x = \dfrac{40}{5} = 8$

12. **(d)** Here, $3(2 - 5p) - 2(1 - 6p) = 1$
$\Rightarrow 6 - 15p - 2 + 12p = 1$
$\Rightarrow 4 - 3p = 1 \Rightarrow 3p = 4 - 1$
$\Rightarrow 3p = 3 \quad \Rightarrow p = \dfrac{3}{3} = 1$

13. **(a)** Let the number be x.
$\therefore 3x - 8 = 13 \Rightarrow 3x = 13 + 8$
$\Rightarrow 3x = 21$
$\Rightarrow x = \dfrac{21}{3} = 7$

14. **(a)** Let the numbers are $x, x + 1, x + 2$.
$\therefore x + x + 1 + x + 2 = 114$
$\Rightarrow 3x + 3 = 114 \Rightarrow 3x = 114 - 3$
$\Rightarrow 3x = 111 \Rightarrow x = \dfrac{111}{3} = 37$
Greatest number $= 37 + 2 = 39$

15. **(c)** Let the breadth be x m.
Length $= (x + 5)$
Perimeter of rectangle $= 74$
$\Rightarrow 2(x + 5 + x) = 74$
$\Rightarrow 2x + 5 = 37 \Rightarrow 2x = 37 - 5$
$\Rightarrow 2x = 32$
$\Rightarrow x = \dfrac{32}{2} = 16$ m
Length $= 16 + 5 = 21$ m

16. **(b)** Let the number be x.
$2x + 9 = 57 \Rightarrow 2x = 57 - 9 = 48$
$x = 24$

17. **(a)** Let the number be x.
$\therefore x - 7 = 37 \Rightarrow x = 37 + 7 = 44$

18. **(d)** Let the age of daughter be x years.
$\therefore$ Man's age $= 3x$.
and 5 years ago, daughter's age $= x - 5$
$\therefore$ Man's age $= 3x - 5$
$\Rightarrow 3x - 5 = 4x - 20 \Rightarrow 4x - 3x = -5 + 20$
$\Rightarrow x = 15$ years

19. **(b)** Let the age of Karan be x years.
Father's age $= 3x$ years
After 14 years,

$$3x + 14 = 2(x - 14)$$
$$\Rightarrow 3x + 14 = 2x + 28$$
$$\Rightarrow x = 28 - 14$$
$$\Rightarrow x = 14 \text{ years}$$

20. **(a)** Let the three consecutive even numbers are

$$x, x + 2, x + 4.$$
$$\therefore x + x + 2 + x + 4 = 78$$
$$\Rightarrow 3x = 78 - 6$$
$$\Rightarrow 3x = 72$$
$$\Rightarrow x = \frac{72}{3} = 24$$

21. **(a)** Let the price of the ratio be ₹ x.
$$\therefore 5x = 170 + 3x$$
$$\Rightarrow 2x = 170$$
$$\Rightarrow x = \frac{170}{2} = 85$$

22. **(b)** Let the breadth be x m

Length = $3x$ m

Perimeter of rectangular park = 168
$$\Rightarrow 2(l + b) = 168$$
$$\Rightarrow 2(3x + x) = 168$$
$$\Rightarrow 8x = 168$$
$$\Rightarrow x = \frac{168}{8} = 21 \text{ m}$$

23. **(c)** Let the number be x.
$$\therefore x \times 17 + 4 = 225$$
$$\Rightarrow 17x = 225 - 4$$
$$\Rightarrow 17x = 221$$
$$\Rightarrow x = \frac{221}{17} = 13$$

24. **(d)** Required result
$$= 3a - 2b + 5c + 2a + 5b - 7c - a - b + c$$
$$= 4a + 2b - c$$

25. **(c)**

26. **(b)** Required result =
$$2a - [3b - \{a - (2c + 3b) + 4c - 3a + 3b + 6c\}]$$
$$= 2a - [3b - \{-2a + 6b + 8c\}]$$
$$= 2a - [3b + 2a - 6b - 8c]$$
$$= 2a - [2a - 3b - 8c] = 2a - 2a + 3b + 8c$$
$$= 3b + 8c$$

27. **(b)** $xy - [yz - zx - \{yx - (3y - xz) - (xy - zy)\}]$
$$= xy - [yz - zx - \{yx - 3y + xz - xy + zy\}]$$
$$= xy - [yz - zx - yx + 3y - xz + xy - zy]$$
$$= xy + 2xz - 3y$$

28. **(d)** Given $\dfrac{x}{8} - \dfrac{1}{2} = \dfrac{x}{6} - 2$
$$\Rightarrow \frac{x}{8} - \frac{x}{6} = \frac{1}{2} - 2$$
$$\Rightarrow \frac{3x - 4x}{24} = \frac{1 - 4}{2}$$
$$\Rightarrow \frac{-x}{24} = \frac{-3}{2} \quad \Rightarrow -2x = -3 \times 24$$
$$\Rightarrow x = 36$$

29. **(a)** Let the number be x.
$$\therefore 3 \times x + 7 = 70$$
$$\Rightarrow 3x = 70 - 7$$
$$\Rightarrow 3x = 63$$
$$\Rightarrow x = \frac{63}{3} = 21.$$

30. **(c)** Let the breadth be x.
$$\therefore \text{Length} = x + 7$$
Perimeter of wire = 86
$$\Rightarrow 2(l + b) = 86$$
$$\Rightarrow l + b = \frac{86}{2}$$
$$\Rightarrow l + b = 43$$
$$\Rightarrow x + 7 + x = 43$$
$$\Rightarrow 2x = 43 - 7$$
$$\Rightarrow 2x = 36$$
$$\Rightarrow x = 18$$
$$\therefore \text{Length} = x + 7 = 18 + 7 = 25 \text{ cm}$$

Area is the measure of surface. To measure area, we need a standard area as a unit of measurement.

Perimeter of a Rectangle and a Square

Perimeter of rectangle = 2 (length + breadth)

$$= 2(l + b)$$

Example 1:   Find the perimeter of the rectangle whose length is 14m and breadth 8m.

    Solution: Here, l = 14m; b = 8m

                     ∴ Perimeter of rectangle = 2 $(l + b)$ = 2 (14 + 8) = 2 × 22 = 44m.

Example 2:   The perimeter of a rectangular field is 110m. If its width is 23m, what is its length?

    Solution: Given, perimeter = 110m.

                           b = 23m

                           l = ?

                 ∴ 2 $(l + b)$ = 110

$$\Rightarrow l + b = \frac{110}{2} = 55$$

                 ⇒ l + 23 = 55

                 ⇒ l = 55 − 23 = 32m

                 ∴ length = 32m

                 Perimeter of a square = 4 × side.

Example 3:   What is the perimeter of a square each of whose sides measures 5.6 cm?

    Solution: Here, a = 5.6 cm

                 ∴ Perimeter of square = 4 × a

                               = 4 × 5.6

                               = 22.4 cm

Example 4:   The cost of fencing a square field at ₹ 35per meter is 4480. What is the length of each side of the square?

    Solution: Perimeter of square field = $\dfrac{4480}{35}$ = 128 m

                   ⇒ $4a$ = 128

                   ⇒ $a = \dfrac{128}{4}$ = 32m

Example 5:   Find the perimeter of a regular pentagon of side 6.4 cm.

    Solution: Perimeter of hexagon = 5 × 6.4 = 32.0 cm

Circumference of a Circle

The perimeter of a circle is called its circumference.

                 Circumference of a circle = $2\pi r$

                 where r = radius of the circle   and $\pi = \dfrac{22}{7}$

Example 6: Find the circumference of a circle of radius 28 cm.

Solution: Here, $r = 28$ cm

∴ Circumference of circle = $2\pi r$

$$= 2 \times \frac{22}{7} \times 28$$
$$= 8 \times 22$$
$$= 176 \text{ cm}$$

Example 7: Find the diameter of the circle whose circumference is 88 cm.

Solution: Circumference of circle = 88

$$\Rightarrow \qquad 2\pi r = 88$$

$$\Rightarrow \quad 2 \times \frac{22}{7} \times r = 88$$

$$\Rightarrow \qquad r = \frac{88 \times 7}{2 \times 22} = 14 \text{ cm}$$

∴ Diameter = $2r = 2 \times 14 = 28$ cm

Area of a Rectangle and a Square

Area of rectangle = length × breadth

and Length = $\dfrac{\text{area of rectangle}}{\text{breadth}}$

and Breadth = $\dfrac{\text{area of rectangle}}{\text{length}}$

Example 8: Find the area of rectangle whose length and breadth are 32cm and 14cm respectively.

Solution: Area of rectangle = $l \times b$
$$= 32 \times 14 = 448 \text{ cm}^2$$

Example 9: The area of rectangle is 630 cm^2 and its length is 35 cm. What is its perimeter?

Solution: Given area of rectangle = 630

$\Rightarrow l \times b = 630$

$\Rightarrow 35 \times b = 630$

$\Rightarrow b = \dfrac{630}{35} = 18$ cm

∴ Perimeter of rectangle = $2(l + b) = 2(35 + 18) = 2 \times 53 = 106$ cm

Area of square = $(\text{side})^2$

Area of square = $\dfrac{1}{2}(\text{diagonal})^2$

Example 10: What is the area of square whose side is 18cm?

Solution: Area of square = $(\text{side})^2 = (18)^2 = 324$ cm^2

Example 11: If the perimeter of square is 48m, what is its area?

Solution: Perimeter of square = 48

$4 \times a = 48 \Rightarrow a = \dfrac{48}{4} = 12$

Area of square = $a^2 = 12^2 = 144$ m^2

---

1. If a wire of length 267 cm be bent to form an equilateral triangle, then what is the length of side of the equilateral triangle?
   (a) 69 cm (b) 79 cm
   (c) 89 cm (d) 99 cm

2. Mohit runs a distance of 7km 800m in going round a rectangular ground three times. What is the length of the ground if its width is 330m?
   (a) 670 m (b) 770 m
   (c) 870 m (d) 970 m

3. What is the perimeter of an isosceles triangles with equal sides 8.5cm each and third side 7cm?
   (a) 12 cm (b) 24 cm
   (c) 13 cm (d) 26 cm

4. What is the perimeter of regular hexagon having each side 6.5 cm ?
   (a) 39 cm (b) 38 cm
   (c) 42 cm (d) 46 cm

5. The cost of fencing a rectangular field at ₹ 18 per metre is ₹ 1980. If the width of the field is 23m, what is its length?
   (a) 36 m (b) 24 m
   (c) 32 m (d) 28 m

6. What is the diameter of the circle whose circumference is 66 cm?
   (a) 18 cm (b) 21 cm
   (c) 23 cm (d) 28 cm

7. What is the radius of the circle whose circumference is 264 cm?
   (a) 36 cm (b) 42cm
   (c) 46 cm (d) 48 cm

8. The diameter of the wheel of a car is 70 cm. How many revolutions will it make to travel 1.65km?
   (a) $6\frac{1}{2}$ (b) $4\frac{1}{2}$
   (c) $7\frac{1}{2}$ (d) $5\frac{1}{2}$

9. What is the circumference of a circle whose diameter is 35cm?
   (a) 110 cm (b) 120 cm
   (c) 105 cm (d) 115 cm

10. The area of a rectangle is 630 cm^2 and its length is 35cm, what is its perimeter?
    (a) 102 cm (b) 104 cm
    (c) 106 cm (d) 108 cm

11. The total cost of flooring a room at ₹ 85/m^2 is ₹ 5100. If the length of the room is 8m, then what is its width?
    (a) 6.5 m (b) 7.5 m
    (c) 8.5 m (d) 8 m

12. The area of a rectangle is 540 cm^2. Its length is 36cm, what is its perimeter?
    (a) 92 cm (b) 102 cm
    (c) 112 cm (d) 118 cm

13. What is the area of square whose diagonal is $5\sqrt{2}$ cm?
    (a) 100 cm^2 (b) $25\sqrt{2}$ cm^2
    (c) 25 cm^2 (d) 50 cm^2

14. The length and breadth of a rectangular park are in the ratio 5 : 3 and its perimeter is 128m. What is the area of the park?
    (a) 960 m^2 (b) 1260 m^2
    (c) 480 m^2 (d) 680 m^2

15. What is the number of square tiles of size 10cm required for decorating a wall of 12 m × 8 m?
    (a) 108000 (b) 9800
    (c) 9600 (d) 9200

16. Five flower beds each of side 3cm are dug on a piece of land 17m long and 5m wide. What is the area of remaining part of the land?
    (a) 35 cm^2 (b) 40 cm^2
    (c) 25 cm^2 (d) 30 cm^2

17. The perimeter of the given figure is 37 cm. find the missing value.

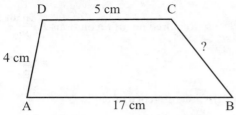

(a) 10 cm   (b) 11 cm

(c) 12 cm   (d) 13 cm

18. The area of a square is 240 cm^2. What is its perimeter?

(a) 184 cm   (b) 192 cm

(c) 196 cm   (d) None of these

19. The diagonal of a square is $8\sqrt{2}$ cm what is its perimeter?

(a) 32 cm   (b) 64 cm

(c) 36 cm   (d) 42 cm

20. A floor is 7m long and 5m wide. A square carpet of sides 4m is laid on the floor. What is the area of floor that is not carpeted?

(a) 15 m^2 (b) 18 m^2

(c) 17 m^2 (d) 19 m^2

21. A room is 7m long and 4m 25cm wide how many square metres of carpet is needed to cover the floor of the room?

(a) 29.15 m^2 (b) 29.25 m^2

(c) 29.5 m^2 (d) 29.75 m^2

22. Find the number of square tiles of size 15cm required for covering the floor of a room 9m long and 6m wide.

(a) 1800   (b) 2400

(c) 1600   (d) 2800

23. A rectangle and square are of equal area. The side of square is 18m. What is the length of rectangle if it is 12m wide?

(a) 23 m   (b) 27 m

(c) 32 m   (d) 22 m

24. What is the cost of tiling a rectangular plot of land 400m and 100m wide at the rate of ₹ 7 per hundred sq. m?

(a) ₹ 5614.285   (b) ₹ 5714.285

(c) ₹ 5724.285   (d) ₹ 5734.285

25. If the length and breadth of a rectangle are doubled then its perimeter is

(a) Halved   (b) Doubled

(c) Tripled   (d) None of these

Answer Key

1. (c)	2. (d)	3. (b)	4. (a)	5. (c)	6. (b)	7. (b)	8. (c)	9. (a)	10 (c)
11. (b)	12. (b)	13. (c)	14. (a)	15. (c)	16. (b)	17. (b)	18. (c)	19. (b)	20. (d)
21. (d)	22. (b)	23. (b)	24. (b)	25. (b)					

1. **(c)** If x is required length then

   $x + x + x = 267$

   $3x = 267 \Rightarrow x = \dfrac{267}{3} = 89$ cm

2. **(d)** Here, $3 \times$ perimeter of rectangular ground
   $= 7800$ m

   $\Rightarrow 3\,[2\,(l + b)] = 7800$

   $\Rightarrow l + 330 = \dfrac{7800}{6}$

   $\Rightarrow l + 330 = 1300$

   $\Rightarrow l = 1300 - 330 = 970$ m

3. **(b)**

   Perimeter of isosceles triangle
   $= 8.5 + 8.5 + 7 = 24$ cm

4. **(a)**

   Perimeter of regular hexagon
   $= 6 \times 6.5$ cm $= 39$ cm

5. **(c)**

   Here, Perimeter $= \dfrac{1980}{18} = 110$ m

   If l and b are its length and breadth, then

   $\Rightarrow 2\,(l + b) = 110$

   $\Rightarrow 2\,(l + 23) = 110$

   $\Rightarrow l + 23 = 55 \Rightarrow l = 55 - 23 = 32$ m

6. **(b)**

   Circumference of circle $= 66$

   $2\pi r = 66$ where r is radius

   $\therefore 2r = \dfrac{66}{\pi} = \dfrac{66}{\frac{22}{7}} = \dfrac{66 \times 7}{22} = 21$ cm

7. **(b)** Given,

   $2\pi r = 264$ where r is radius

   $\therefore r = \dfrac{264}{2 \times \pi} = \dfrac{264 \times 7}{2 \times 22} = 42$ cm

8. **(c)** Circumference of wheel of car

   $= 2\pi r = 2 \times \dfrac{22}{7} \times \dfrac{70}{2} = 220$ m

$\therefore$ Required no. of revolutions $= \dfrac{1650}{220}$

$= 7\dfrac{1}{2}$

9. **(a)** Circumference of circle

   $2\pi r = \dfrac{22}{7} \times 35 = 22 \times 5 = 110$ cm

10. **(c)**

    If b is breadth of rectangle then

    $35 \times b = 630 \Rightarrow b = \dfrac{630}{35} = 18$ cm

    Perimeter $= 2\,(l + b) = 2\,(35 + 18)$
    $= 2 \times 53 = 106$ cm

11. **(b)**

    Area of the room $= \dfrac{5100}{85} = 60$ m^2

    If b is its width then

    $l \times b = 60$

    $8 \times b = 60 \Rightarrow b = \dfrac{60}{8} = 7.5$ m

12. **(b)** Breadth of rectangle

    $b = \dfrac{540}{36} = 15$ cm

    $\therefore$ Perimeter of rectangle $= 2\,(36 + 15)$
    $= 2 \times 51 = 102$ cm.

13. **(c)**

    Area of square $= \dfrac{1}{2} \times \left(5\sqrt{2}\right)^2$

    $= \dfrac{1}{2} \times 25 \times 2$

    $= 25$ cm^2

14. **(a)** If $5x$ and $3x$ are length and breadth then
    $2\,(5x + 3x) = 128$

    $\Rightarrow x = \dfrac{128}{16} = 8$

    $\therefore l = 5 \times 8 = 40$ m

    and $b = 3 \times 8 = 24$ m

    Hence, area $= l \times b = 40 \times 24 = 960$ m^2

15. **(c)** Required no. of square tiles

$$= \frac{12 \times 100 \times 8 \times 100}{10 \times 10}$$

$$= 9600$$

16. **(b)** Area of one flower bed = 3 × 3

$$= 9 \text{ cm}^2$$

Area of five flower beds = 9 × 5 = 45 cm^2

Area of rectangular field = 17 × 5

$$= 85 \text{ cm}^2$$

Area of remaining part = 85 – 45

$$= 40 \text{ cm}^2$$

17. **(b)** Missing value = 37 – (5 + 4 + 17)

$$= 37 - 26 = 11 \text{ cm}$$

18. **(c)** Area of square = 2401 = 49 × 49

∴ Side of square = 49 cm

Hence, perimeter of square

$$= 4 \times \text{side} = 4 \times 49 = 196 \text{ cm}$$

19. **(a)** Area of square = $\frac{1}{2}$ × (diagonal)^2

$$= \frac{1}{2} \times \left(8\sqrt{2}\right)^2$$

$$= \frac{1}{2} \times 64 \times 2$$

$$= 64$$

∴ Side of square = 8 cm

Hence, perimeter of square

$$= 4 \times 8 = 32 \text{ cm}$$

20. **(d)** Area of floor = 7 × 5 = 35 m^2

Area of carpet = 4 × 4 = 16 m^2

Remaining part = 35 – 16 = 19 m^2

21. **(d)** Area of floor = $7 \times 4\frac{25}{100}$

$$= 7 \times 4\frac{1}{4}$$

$$= 7 \times \frac{17}{4}$$

$$= 29.75 \text{ m}^2$$

22. **(b)** Required no. of square tiles

$$= \frac{9 \times 100 \times 6 \times 100}{15 \times 15}$$

$$= 3 \times 2 \times 20 \times 20$$

$$= 2400$$

23. **(b)** Given, Area of rectangle = area of square

$$\Rightarrow \quad l \times 12 = (18)^2$$

$$\Rightarrow \quad l = \frac{18 \times 18}{12} = 27 \text{ m}$$

24. **(b)** Cost of tiling = $\frac{400 \times 100}{7} = \frac{40000}{7}$

$$= ₹ 5714.285$$

25. **(b)** Perimeter = 2 (l + b)

New perimeter = 2 (2l + 2b)

$$= 2 \times 2 (l + b)$$

$$= 4 (l + b)$$

$$= 2 [2 (l + b)]$$

Point

A dimensionless line is called a point. Point is basically an undefined term. It is the fundamental object of Geometry.

Line

A line is formed by joining two points, or joining of two points forms a line. A line has no end points and a line has infinite points. The symbol for the line AB is $\overleftrightarrow{AB}$.

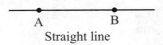

Straight line

Line Segment

A line having fixed end points and fixed length is called a line segment. A line segment has two fixed points. The symbol for the line segment AB is $\overline{AB}$.

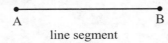

line segment

Ray

A ray is a line whose one end is fixed and other is not fixed.

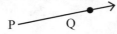

PQ is a ray. A ray is represented by $\overrightarrow{PQ}$.
In ray PQ, P is fixed point and Q is not fixed.

Plane

Every solid has a surface. A surface may be flat or curved.

Example: A cone has 2 surfaces. In the figure 1st surface, i.e., surface 1 is curved and surface 2 is flat surface.

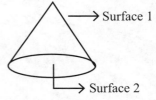

Incidence properties in a plane:

(1) An unlimited number of lines can be drawn passing through a given point.

(2) Exactly one and only one line can be drawn passing through two different given points in a plane.

Intersecting and Parallel Lines

If there is a common point to two given lines then these lines are called intersecting lines.

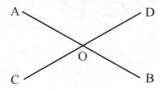

In above figure, AB and CD are intersecting lines in which O is the common point. If no point is common to two given lines, then the two lines are called parallel lines.

Example: The rails of a railway line, opposite sides of rectangle.

A ———————— B

C ———————— D

AB and CD are parallel lines.

Concurrent Lines

Three or more lines in a plane, all of which pass through the same point are called concurrent lines.

Some important points:

1. A line has no end points.
2. A ray has one end point.
3. A line segment has two end points.
4. Two planes intersect in a line.
5. Two lines intersect at a point.
6. The minimum number of point of intersection of three lines in a plane is zero.

Angle

The figure formed by two rays with the same initial point is called an angle.

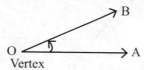

The common initial point is called vertex. The rays forming the angle are called the arms or sides.

Interior of an Angle

All those points which lie inside the angle are called interior of the angle.

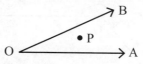

The point P is interior of ∠AOB.

Exterior of an Angle

All those points which lie outside the angle form the exterior of the angle.

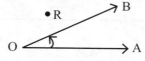

The point R is exterior of ∠AOB.

Types of Angles

(1) **Right angle:** An angle whose measure is 90° is called a right angle.

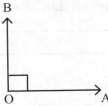

(2) **Acute angle:** An angle whose measure is more than 0° but less than 90° is called an acute angle.

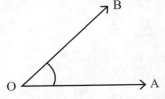

(3) **Obtuse angle:** An angle whose measure is more than 90° but less than 180° is called obtuse angle.

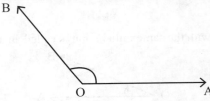

(4) **Straight angle:** An angle whose measure is 180° is called a straight line.

(5) **Reflex angle:** An angle whose measure is more than 180° but less than 360° is called a reflex angle.

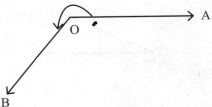

(6) **Complete angle:** An angle whose measure is 360° is called a complete angle.

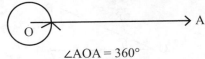

∠AOA = 360°

Closed Figure: A figure which begins and ends at the same point is called closed figure.

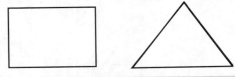

Open Figure: A figure which does not end at the starting point is called an open figure.

Polygon: A closed figure formed by three or more line segments is called polygon.

Sides: The line segments forming a polygon are called sides.

Vertices: The meeting point of a pair of sides of a polygon is called vertex.

Adjacent sides: Any two sides of a polygon having a common end point are called adjacent sides.

Diagonals: A line segment joining two non adjacent vertices are called diagonals.

Triangle: A polygon having 3 sides.

Quadrilateral: A polygon having 4 sides.

Pentagon: A polygon having 5 sides.

Hexagon: A polygon having 6 sides.

Octagon: A polygon having 8 sides.

   Note: The no. of sides and no. of angles in a polygon is same.

Types of Triangle

According to the sides, the triangle has three types:

   (1) **Scalene triangle:** A triangle whose all sides are different.

   (2) **Isosceles triangle:** A triangle whose two sides are equal.

   (3) **Equilateral triangle:** A triangle whose all sides are equal.

According to the angles, triangles have three types.

   (1) **Acute triangle:** A triangle each of whose angle measures less than 90°.

   (2) **Right triangle:** A triangle whose one angle measures 90°.

   (3) **Obtuse triangle:** A triangle whose one of the angle measures more than 90°.

Important Points

   (1) The sum of all angles of a triangle is 180°.

   (2) The sum of all sides of a triangle is called its perimeter.

   (3) A triangle cannot have more than one right angle.

   (4) A triangle cannot have more than one obtuse angle.

   (5) In a right triangle, the sum of two acute angles is 90°.

   (6) The angles opposite to equal sides of an isosceles triangles are equal.

   (7) Each angle of an equilateral triangle is 60°.

   (8) The sum of angles of a quadrilateral is 360°.

Example 1: One of the base angle of an isosceles triangle is 68°. Find the other two angles.

Solution: Here,

$\angle ABC = \angle ACB = 68°$

$\therefore \angle BAC = 180° - (68° + 68°)$

$= 180° - 136° = 44°$

Example 2: Two sides of a triangle are 6cm and 8cm. Its perimeter is 25cm. what is its third side?

Solution:

Perimeter of triangle = 25cm

$\Rightarrow 6 + 8 + x = 25$

$\Rightarrow x = 25 - 14 = 11$ cm

Example 3: How many degrees are in $\dfrac{2}{3}$ right angle.

Solution:

$\dfrac{2}{3}$ right angle $= \dfrac{2}{3} \times 90° = 60°$

Example 4: What is the value of x in the figure given below?

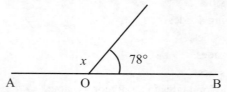

Solution: Here, $\angle AOB = 180°$

$\Rightarrow x + 78° = 180°$

$\Rightarrow x = 180° - 78° = 102°$

Example 5: The angles of a triangle are in the ratio 5 : 6 : 7. What is the measure of largest angle?

Solution: Here,

$5x + 6x + 7x = 180°$

$\Rightarrow \qquad 18x = 180°$

$\Rightarrow \qquad x = \dfrac{180°}{18} = 10°$

$\therefore$ largest angle = $7x = 7 \times 10° = 70°$

Example 6: The angles of a quadrilateral are in the ratio 7 : 8 : 10 : 11. What is the measure of largest angle?

Solution:

$7x + 8x + 10x + 11x = 360°$

$\Rightarrow \qquad 36x = 360°$

$\Rightarrow \qquad x = \dfrac{360°}{36} = 10°$

$\therefore$ largest angle = $11x = 11 \times 10 = 110°$

1. How many degrees are there in four right angles?
   (a) 180°   (b) 270°
   (c) 360°   (d) None of these

2. How many degrees are there in the angle between the hour hand and the minute hand of a clock when it is 3 O'clock?
   (a) 60°   (b) 90°
   (c) 180°   (d) 120°

3. How many rays can be drawn with a given point as the initial point?
   (a) One
   (b) Two
   (c) Four
   (d) An unlimited number

4. The maximum number of points of intersection of three lines in a plane is
   (a) 0   (b) 1
   (c) 2   (d) 3

5. Which of the following has no end points?
   (a) A ray   (b) A line
   (c) A line segment   (d) An angle

6. How many lines can be drawn passing through two given points?
   (a) One
   (b) Two
   (c) Three
   (d) Unlimited number

7. A square has
   (a) One line of symmetry
   (b) Two lines of symmetry
   (c) Three lines of symmetry
   (d) Four lines of symmetry

8. A circle has
   (a) One line of symmetry
   (b) No lines of symmetry
   (c) An unlimited number of lines of symmetry
   (d) Two lines of symmetry

9. Which of the following statement is true?
   (a) A square has four lines of symmetry
   (b) A parallelogram has no lines of symmetry
   (c) A rhombus has four lines of symmetry
   (d) A rectangle has four lines of symmetry.

10. A cuboid has
    (a) Length only
    (b) Thickness only
    (c) Length and breadth only
    (d) Length, breadth and height

11. The sum of all angles of a quadrilateral is
    (a) 180°   (b) 270°
    (c) 360°   (d) 540°

12. A quadrilateral having one and only one pair of parallel sides is
    (a) A kite
    (b) A rhombus
    (c) A trapezium
    (d) A parallelogram

13. How many parts does a triangle have?
    (a) 2   (b) 3
    (c) 6   (d) 9

14. The angle of a triangle are in the ratio 2 : 3 : 4. The smallest angle is
    (a) 40°   (b) 60°
    (c) 80°   (d) None of these

15. One of the base angle of an isosceles triangle is 65°. The vertical angle is
    (a) 40°   (b) 50°
    (c) 65°   (d) 35°

16. Each angle of an equilateral triangle is
    (a) 30°   (b) 45°
    (c) 60°   (d) 80°

17. An angle measuring 360° is
    (a) A straight angle
    (b) A complete angle
    (c) An obtuse angle
    (d) A reflex angle

18. The measure of a straight angle is
    (a) 60°   (b) 90°
    (c) 180°   (d) 360°

19. An angle measuring 205° is
    (a) An acute angle
    (b) An obtuse angle
    (c) A reflex angle
    (d) None of these

20. If there are 36 spokes in a bicycle wheel then the angle between a pair of adjacent spokes is
    (a) 10°   (b) 12°
    (c) 15°   (d) 18°

21. The minimum number of points of intersection of three lines in a plane is
    (a) 0   (b) 1
    (c) 2   (d) 3

22. Two planes intersect
    (a) In a plane   (b) At a point
    (c) In a line   (d) None of these

23. One of the acute angle of a right triangle is 55°. What is the other acute angle?
    (a) 45°   (b) 35°
    (c) 25°   (d) 55°

24. In a ∆ABC, $3\angle A = 4\angle B = 6\angle C$. What is the measure of largest angle?
    (a) 80°   (b) 60°
    (c) 40°   (d) None of these

25. A triangle having sides of different length is called
    (a) A scalene triangle
    (b) A right triangle
    (c) An isosceles triangle
    (d) An equilateral triangle

26. The angles of a quadrilateral are in the ratio 3 : 4 : 5 : 6. What is the largest angle
    (a) 80°   (b) 102°
    (c) 120°   (d) 150°

27. A quadrilateral having two pairs of equal adjacent sides but unequal opposite sides is
    (a) Square   (b) Rectangle
    (c) Kite   (d) Trapezium

28. A cone has how many vertex?
    (a) 1   (b) 2
    (c) 3   (d) None of these

29. A brick is an example of
    (a) Cube   (b) Prism
    (c) Cylinder   (d) Cuboid

30. How many vertex a cylinder has?
    (a) 0   (b) 1
    (c) 2   (d) 3

Answer Key

1. (c)	2. (b)	3. (d)	4. (d)	5. (c)	6. (a)	7. (d)	8. (c)	9. (a)	10 (d)
11. (c)	12. (c)	13. (c)	14. (a)	15. (b)	16. (c)	17. (b)	18. (c)	19. (c)	20. (a)
21. (a)	22. (c)	23. (b)	24. (a)	25. (a)	26. (c)	27. (b)	28. (a)	29. (d)	30. (a)

1. **(c)**

   $4 \times 90° = 360°$

2. **(b)**

   Required degrees $= \dfrac{3}{12} \times 360° = 90°$

14. **(a)** Here,

    $2x + 3x + 4x = 180°$

    $\Rightarrow 9x = 180° \Rightarrow x = \dfrac{180°}{9} = 20°$

    Smallest angle $= 2x = 2 \times 20° = 40°$

15. **(b)**

    Vertical angle $= 180° - (65° + 65°)$

    $= 180° - 130° = 50°$

20. **(a)**

    Required angle $= \dfrac{360°}{36} = 10°$

23. **(b)**

    Other angle $= 180° - (90° + 55°)$

    $= 180° - 145° = 35°$

24. **(a)**

    Here, $\angle A + \angle B + \angle C = 180°$

    $\Rightarrow 3\angle A = 4\angle B = 6\angle C$

    $\Rightarrow \dfrac{3\angle A}{12} = \dfrac{4\angle B}{12} = \dfrac{6\angle C}{12} = x$

    $\Rightarrow \angle A = 4x; \ \angle B = 3x; \ \angle C = 2x$

    $\therefore 4x + 3x + 2x = 180° \Rightarrow 9x = 180° \Rightarrow x = 20°$

    Hence, $\angle A = 4 \times 20° = 80°$

26. **(c)**

    $3x + 4x + 5x + 6x = 360°$

    $\Rightarrow 18x = 360° \Rightarrow x = \dfrac{360°}{18} = 20°$

    $\therefore$ Largest angle $= 6 \times 20° = 120°$

Section 2
LOGICAL
REASONING

In these types of questions, a set of figures and arrangement or a matrix in given, each of which has a certain characters, be it numbers, letters or a group or combination of letters or numbers, follow a certain pattern. The candidate is required to analyse the pattern and find the missing character in the figure.

In pattern, the missing character is obtained by adding, subtracting, multiplying, or dividing by some number after going through the pattern. In the figure type, the middle term is the addition of all the given terms or addition of squares of each term or square of addition of all given terms.

Sometimes the left part of figure has exactly the same relation as the right part of the figure. The candidate is required to find the certain rule to find the missing character. He/she should know various mathematical operations, squares, cubes etc. and relate them accordingly.

Example 1:

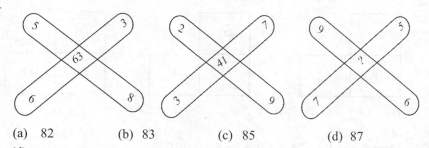

    (a) 82   (b) 83   (c) 85   (d) 87

Solution: (d)

From figure 1 $6 \times 8 + 5 \times 3 = 48 + 15 = 63$

From figure 2 $3 \times 9 + 2 \times 7 = 27 + 14 = 41$

From figure 3 $7 \times 6 + 9 \times 5 = 42 + 45 = 87$

Example 2:

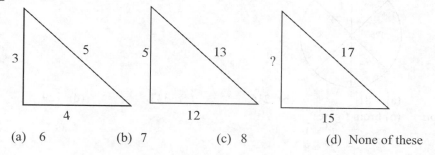

    (a) 6   (b) 7   (c) 8   (d) None of these

Solution: (c)
From figure 1 $3^2 + 4^2 = 5^2$
From figure 2 $5^2 + 12^2 = 13^2$
From figure 3 $8^2 + 15^2 = 17^2$ ∴ ? = 8

Example 3:

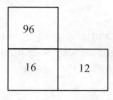 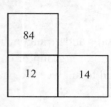 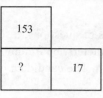

(a) 15 (b) 16 (c) 18 (d) None of these

Solution: (c) From figure 1 $(16) \times \left(\dfrac{12}{2}\right) = 16 \times 6 = 96$ From figure 2 $\left(12 \times \dfrac{14}{2}\right) = 12 \times 7 = 84$

From figure 3 $? \times \dfrac{17}{2} = 153$ ⇒ $? = 2 \times 9 \Rightarrow 18$

Example 4:

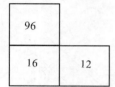 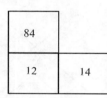 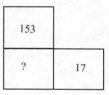

(a) 14 (b) 16 (c) 17 (d) 18

Solution: (d)
From figure 1 $(96 \div 12) \times 2 = 8 \times 2 = 16$
From figure 2 $(84 \div 14) \times 2 = 6 \times 2 = 12$
From figure 3 $(153 \div 17) \times 2 = 9 \times 2 = 18$

Example 5:

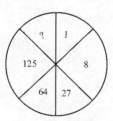

(a) 81 (b) 216 (c) 343 (d) 729

Solution: (b) From figure
$$1^3 = 1$$
$$2^3 = 8$$
$$3^3 = 27$$
$$4^3 = 64$$
$$5^3 = 125$$
$$6^3 = 216$$

Study the pattern and find the missing number.

1.

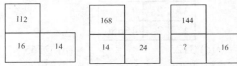

(a) 14   (b) 16

(c) 18   (d) 21

2.

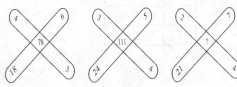

(a) 98   (b) 96

(c) 99   (d) 108

3.

(a) 121   (b) 149

(c) 169   (d) 196

4.

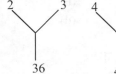

(a) 1594   (b) 1764

(c) 1664   (d) 1784

5.

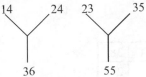

(a) 75   (b) 76

(c) 77   (d) 78

6.

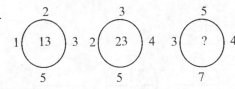

(a) 43   (b) 45

(c) 46   (d) 47

7.

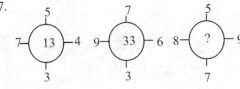

(a) 35   (b) 36

(c) 37   (d) 38

8.

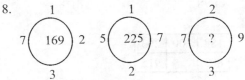

(a) 361   (b) 324

(c) 441   (d) 484

9.

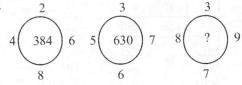

(a) 1512   (b) 1412

(c) 1212   (d) 1312

10.

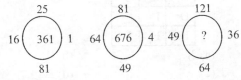

(a) 961   (b) 964

(c) 1024   (d) 1044

11.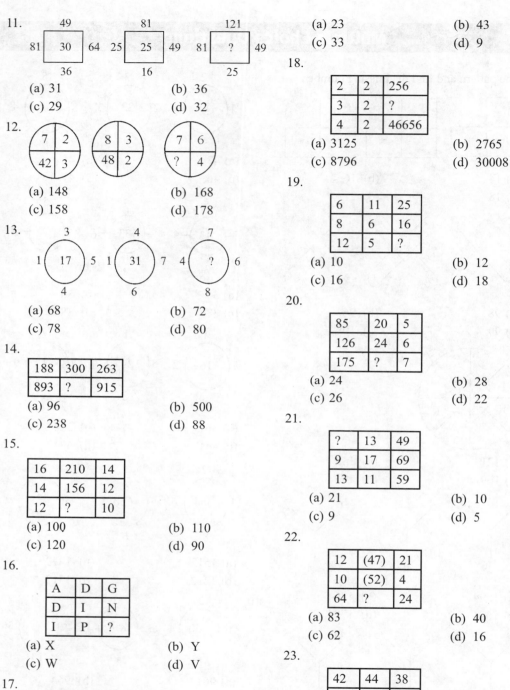

| 49 | | 81 | | 121 | |
81 | 30 | 64   25 | 25 | 49   81 | ? | 49
| 36 | | 16 | | 25 | |

(a) 31   (b) 36
(c) 29   (d) 32

12.
| 7 | 2 | | 8 | 3 | | 7 | 6 |
|42 | 3 | |48 | 2 | | ? | 4 |

(a) 148   (b) 168
(c) 158   (d) 178

13.
  3   4   7
1 (17) 5   1 (31) 7   4 (?) 6
  4   6   8

(a) 68   (b) 72
(c) 78   (d) 80

14.
| 188 | 300 | 263 |
| 893 | ? | 915 |

(a) 96   (b) 500
(c) 238   (d) 88

15.
16	210	14
14	156	12
12	?	10

(a) 100   (b) 110
(c) 120   (d) 90

16.
A	D	G
D	I	N
I	P	?

(a) X   (b) Y
(c) W   (d) V

17.
8	17	33
12	5	29
10	13	?

(a) 23   (b) 43
(c) 33   (d) 9

18.
2	2	256
3	2	?
4	2	46656

(a) 3125   (b) 2765
(c) 8796   (d) 30008

19.
6	11	25
8	6	16
12	5	?

(a) 10   (b) 12
(c) 16   (d) 18

20.
85	20	5
126	24	6
175	?	7

(a) 24   (b) 28
(c) 26   (d) 22

21.
?	13	49
9	17	69
13	11	59

(a) 21   (b) 10
(c) 9   (d) 5

22.
12	(47)	21
10	(52)	4
64	?	24

(a) 83   (b) 40
(c) 62   (d) 16

23.
42	44	38
23	55	28
37	?	39

(a) 77   (b) 22
(c) 33   (d) 66

24.

963	2	844
464	?	903

(a) 4　　　　　　　　　　(b) 2

(c) 1　　　　　　　　　　(d) 3

25.

3	4	5
3	7	12
3	?	22

(a) 9　　　　　　　　　　(b) 11

(c) 10　　　　　　　　　(d) 8

Answer Key

1. (c)	2. (a)	3. (c)	4. (b)	5. (a)	6. (d)	7. (c)	8. (c)	9. (a)	10 (c)
11. (d)	12. (b)	13. (d)	14. (c)	15. (b)	16. (a)	17. (c)	18. (a)	19. (c)	20. (b)
21. (d)	22. (a)	23. (b)	24. (b)	25. (c)					

Hints and Solutions

1. (c)
From figure 1 $(112 \div 14) \times 2 = 16$
From figure 2 $(168 \div 24) \times 2 = 14$
From figure 3 $(144 \div 16) \times 2 = 9 \times 2 = 18$

2. (a)
From figure 1 $4 \times 6 + 18 \times 3 = 24 + 54 = 78$
From figure 2 $3 \times 5 + 24 \times 4 = 15 + 96 = 111$
From figure 3 $2 \times 7 + 21 \times 4 = 14 + 84 = 98$

3. (c)
From figure I $1 + 2 = 3 \rightarrow 3^2 = 9$
From figure II $3 + 4 = 7 \rightarrow 7^2 = 49$
$\qquad 5 + 4 = 9 \rightarrow 9^2 = 81$
$\qquad 7 + 6 = 13 \rightarrow 13^2 = 169$

4. (b)
From figure I $2^2 \times 3^2 = 4 \times 9 = 36$
From figure II $4^2 \times 5^2 = 16 \times 25 = 400$
From figure III $6^2 \times 7^2 = 36 \times 49 = 1764$

5. (a)
From figure I $(14 + 24) - 2 = 38 - 2 = 36$
From figure II $(23 + 35) - 3 = 58 - 3 = 55$
From figure III $(34 + 45) - 4 = 79 - 4 = 75$

6. (d)
From figure I $5 \times 2 + 1 \times 3 = 10 + 3 = 13$
From figure II $2 \times 4 + 5 \times 3 = 8 + 15 = 23$
From figure III $3 \times 4 + 5 \times 7 = 12 + 35 = 47$

7. (c)
From figure I $7 \times 4 - 5 \times 3 = 28 - 15 = 13$
From figure II $9 \times 6 - 7 \times 3 = 54 - 21 = 33$
From figure III $8 \times 9 - 7 \times 5 = 72 - 35 = 37$

8. (c)
From figure I $1 + 7 + 3 + 2 = 13 \rightarrow 13^2 = 169$
From figure II $1 + 5 + 2 + 7 = 15 \rightarrow 15^2 = 225$
From figure III $2 + 7 + 3 + 9 = 21 \rightarrow 21^2$
$\qquad\qquad\qquad\qquad\qquad = 441$

9. (a)
$2 \times 4 \times 8 \times 6 = 384$
$3 \times 5 \times 6 \times 7 = 630$
$3 \times 8 \times 7 \times 9 = 1512$

10. (c)
From figure I $\sqrt{25} + \sqrt{16} + \sqrt{81} + \sqrt{1}$
$\qquad = 5 + 4 + 9 + 1 = 19 \rightarrow 19^2 = 361$
From figure II $\sqrt{81} + \sqrt{64} + \sqrt{49} + \sqrt{4}$
$\qquad = 9 + 8 + 7 + 2 = 26 \rightarrow 26^2 = 676$
From figure III $\sqrt{121} + \sqrt{49} + \sqrt{64} + \sqrt{36}$
$\qquad = 11 + 7 + 8 + 6 = 32 \rightarrow 32^2 = 1024$

11. (d)
From figure I $\sqrt{49} + \sqrt{81} + \sqrt{36} + \sqrt{64}$
$\qquad = 7 + 9 + 6 + 8 = 30$
From figure II $\sqrt{81} + \sqrt{25} + \sqrt{16} + \sqrt{49}$
$\qquad = 9 + 5 + 4 + 7 = 25$
From figure III $\sqrt{121} + \sqrt{81} + \sqrt{25} + \sqrt{49}$
$\qquad = 11 + 9 + 5 + 7 = 32$

12. (b)
From figure I $7 \times 2 \times 3 = 42$
From figure II $8 \times 3 \times 2 = 48$
From figure III $7 \times 6 \times 4 = 168$

13. (d)
From figure I $1 \times 5 + 3 \times 4 = 5 + 12 = 17$
From figure II $1 \times 7 + 4 \times 6 = 7 + 24 = 31$
From figure III $4 \times 6 + 7 \times 8 = 24 + 56 = 80$

14. (c)
In the first row, $(263 - 188) \times 4 = 300$
In the second row, missing number
$\qquad = (915 - 893) \times 4 = 22 \times 4 = 88$

15. (b)
In the first row, $16 \times 14 - 14 = 210$
In the second row, $14 \times 12 - 12 = 156$
$\therefore$ Missing number $= 12 \times 10 - 10 = 110$

16. (a)

17. (c)
In the first row, $8 \times 2 + 17 = 33°$,
in the second row; $12 \times 2 + 5 = 29$
$\therefore$ Missing number $= 10 \times 2 + 13 = 33$

18. (a)
In the first row, $2 + 2 = 4$ and $4^4 = 256$
In the third row, $4 + 2 = 6$ and $6^6 = 46656$

In the second row, $3 + 2 = 5$

So, missing number $= 5^5 = 3125$

19. **(c)**

In the first row, $11 \times 2 + (6 \div 2) = 25$

In the second row, $6 \times 2 + (8 \div 2) = 16$

∴ In the third row, missing number

$= 5 \times 2 + (12 \div 2) = 10 + 6 = 16$

20. **(b)**

In the first row, $(85 \div 5) + 3 = 20$

In the second row, $(126 \div 6) + 3 = 24$

∴ In the third row, missing number

$= (175 \div 7) + 3$

$= (25 + 3) = 28$

21. **(d)**

In the second row, $2 \times 9 + 3 \times 17 = 69$

In the third row, $2 \times 13 + 3 \times 11 = 59$.

Let the missing number in the first row be x.

Then, $2x + 3 \times 13 = 49 \Rightarrow 2x = 10 \Rightarrow x = 5$

22. **(a)**

In the first row, $\dfrac{12}{4} = \dfrac{21}{7}$ in the second row,

$\dfrac{10}{5} = \dfrac{4}{2}$

Clearly, in the third row we have $\dfrac{64}{8} = \dfrac{24}{3}$

∴ Missing number $= 83$

23. **(b)**

In the first row, $(42 - 38) \times 11 = 44$

In the second row, $(28 - 23) \times 11 = 55$

In the third row, missing number

$= (39 - 37) \times 11 = 22$

24. **(b)**

In the first row, $(9 + 6 + 3) - (8 + 4 + 4) = 2$

∴ In the second row, missing number

$= (4 + 6 + 4) - (9 + 0 + 3) = 2$

25. **(c)**

$3 + 4 =$ number below $4 = 7$

$3 + 4 + 5 =$ number below $5 = 12$

$3 + 7 + 12 =$ number below $12 = 22$

∴ Missing number $= 3 + 7 = 10$

2 Analogy

Analogy means similarity. In this type of questions, two objects related in some way are given and third object is also given with four or five alternatives. The student has to find out the alternative that bears the same relation with the third object as the first and second objects have.

This type of questions covers all types of relationship that one can think of. There are many ways of establishing a relationship; some common are given here.

Example 1:   Curd : Milk :: Shoe : ?

   (a) Leather   (b) Cloth
   (c) Jute   (d) Silver

   Solution: As curd is made from milk similarly shoe is made from leather.
   Option (a) is correct.

Example 2:   Calf : Piglet :: Shed : ?

   (a) Prison   (b) Nest
   (c) Pigsty   (d) Den

   Solution: Calf is young one of the cow and piglet is the young of Pig. Shed is the dwelling place of cow. Similarly Pigsty is the dwelling place of pig.
   Option (c) is correct.

Example 3:   Malaria : Mosquito :: ? : ?

   (a) Poison : Death
   (b) Cholera : Water
   (c) Rat : Plague
   (d) Medicine : Disease

   Solution: As malaria is caused due to mosquito, similarly cholera is caused due to water.
   Option (b) is correct.

Example 4:   ABC : ZYX :: CBA : ?

   (a) XYZ   (b) BCA
   (c) YZX   (d) ZXY

   Solution: CBA is the reverse of ABC, similarly XYZ is the reverse of ZYX.
   Option (a) is correct.

Example 5:   4 : 18 :: 6 : ?

   (a) 32   (b) 38
   (c) 11   (d) 37

   Solution: As, $(4)^2 + 2 = 18$
   Similarly, $(6)^2 + 2 = 38$

   Option (b) is correct.

Verbal Analogy

Type1: Complete the analogous pair

Direction (1 to 20):

In each of the following questions, there is a certain relationship between two given words on one side of : : and one word is given on the other side of : : Find out the word from the given alternatives, having the same relation with this word as the words of the given pair bear.

1. Physician : Treatment :: Judge : ?
   - (a) Punishment
   - (b) Judgement
   - (c) Lawyer
   - (d) Court

2. Ice : Coldness :: Earth : ?
   - (a) Weight
   - (b) Jungle
   - (c) Gravity
   - (d) Sea

3. Race : Fatigue :: Fast : ?
   - (a) Food
   - (b) Laziness
   - (c) Hunger
   - (d) Race

4. Peace : Chaos :: Creation : ?
   - (a) Build
   - (b) Construction
   - (c) Destruction
   - (d) Manufacture

5. Tiger : Forest :: Otter : ?
   - (a) Cage
   - (b) Sky
   - (c) Nest
   - (d) Water

6. Poles : Magnet :: ? : Battery
   - (a) Cells
   - (b) Power
   - (c) Terminals
   - (d) Energy

7. Cassock : Priest :: ? : Graduate
   - (a) Cap
   - (b) Tie
   - (c) Coat
   - (d) Gown

8. Country : President :: State : ?
   - (a) Governor
   - (b) M.P.
   - (c) Legislator
   - (d) Minister

9. Cloth : Mill :: Newspaper : ?
   - (a) Editor
   - (b) Reader
   - (c) Paper
   - (d) Press

10. South : North-West :: West : ?
    - (a) North
    - (b) South-West
    - (c) North-East
    - (d) East

11. Tree : Forest :: Grass : ?
    - (a) Lawn
    - (b) Garden
    - (c) Park
    - (d) Field

12. College : Student :: Hospital : ?
    - (a) Nurse
    - (b) Doctor
    - (c) Treatment
    - (d) Patient

13. Conference : Chairman :: Newspaper : ?
    - (a) Reporter
    - (b) Distributor
    - (c) Printer
    - (d) Editor

14. Microphone : Loud :: Microscope : ?
    - (a) Elongate
    - (b) Investigate
    - (c) Magnify
    - (d) Examine

15. Melt : Liquid :: Freeze : ?
    - (a) Ice
    - (b) Condense
    - (c) Solid
    - (d) Force

16. $123 : 13^2 :: 235 : ?$
    - (a) 23^2
    - (b) 35^2
    - (c) 25^3
    - (d) 27^3

17. 14 : 9 :: 26 : ?
    - (a) 12
    - (b) 13
    - (c) 31
    - (d) 15

18. $M \times N : 13 \times 14 :: F \times R : ?$
    - (a) 14×15
    - (b) 5×17
    - (c) 6×18
    - (d) 7×19

19. 16 : 56 :: 32 : ?
    - (a) 96
    - (b) 112
    - (c) 120
    - (d) 128

20. 4 : 19 :: 7 : ?
    - (a) 52
    - (b) 49
    - (c) 28
    - (d) 68

21. 24 : 60 :: 120 : ?
    - (a) 160
    - (b) 220
    - (c) 300
    - (d) 108

22. 335 : 216 :: 987 : ?
    - (a) 868
    - (b) 867
    - (c) 872
    - (d) 888

23. 8 : 24 :: ? : 32
   (a) 5   (b) 6
   (c) 10   (d) 8

24. 9 : 8 :: 16 : ?
   (a) 27   (b) 17
   (c) 16   (d) 18

25. K/T : 11/20 :: J/R : ?
   (a) 10/18   (b) 11/19
   (c) 10/8   (d) 9/10

Type 2: Choosing the analogous pair

Direction (26 to 50):

Each of the following questions consists of two words that have a certain relationship with each other, followed by four lettered pairs of words. Select the lettered pair which has the same relationship as the original pair of words.

26. AERIE : EAGLE
   (a) capital : government
   (b) bridge : architect
   (c) unit : apartment
   (d) house : person

27. PROFESSOR : ERUDITE
   (a) aviator : licensed
   (b) inventor : imaginative
   (c) procrastinator : conscientious
   (d) overseer : wealthy

28. DELTOID : MUSCLE
   (a) radius : bone
   (b) brain : nerve
   (c) tissue : organ
   (d) blood : vein

29. JAUNDICE : LIVER
   (a) rash : skin
   (b) dialysis : kidney
   (c) smog : lung
   (d) valentine : heart

30. CONVICTION : INCARCERATION
   (a) reduction : diminution
   (b) induction : amelioration
   (c) radicalization : estimation
   (d) marginalization : intimidation

31. DEPENDABLE : CAPRICIOUS
   (a) fallible : cantankerous
   (b) erasable : obtuse
   (c) malleable : limpid
   (d) capable : inept

32. METAPHOR : SYMBOL
   (a) pentameter : poem
   (b) rhythm : melody
   (c) nuance : song
   (d) analogy : comparison

33. INTEREST : OBSESSION
   (a) mood : feeling
   (b) weeping : sadness
   (c) dream : fantasy
   (d) plan : negation

34. CONDUCTOR : ORCHESTRA
   (a) jockey : mount
   (b) thrasher : hay
   (c) driver : tractor
   (d) skipper : crew

35. FROND : PALM
   (a) quill : porcupine
   (b) blade : evergreen
   (c) scale : wallaby
   (d) tusk : alligator

36. SOUND : CACOPHONY
   (a) taste : style
   (b) touch : massage
   (c) smell : stench
   (d) sight : panorama

37. UMBRAGE : OFFENSE
   (a) confusion : penance
   (b) infinity : meaning
   (c) decorum : decoration
   (d) elation : jubilance

38. DIRGE : FUNERAL
   (a) chain : letter
   (b) bell : church
   (c) telephone : call
   (d) jingle : commercial

39. PHOBIC : FEARFUL
   (a) cautious : emotional
   (b) envious : desiring
   (c) shy : familiar
   (d) asinine : silly

40. FERAL : TAME
   (a) repetitive : recurrent
   (b) nettlesome : annoying
   (c) repentant : honourable
   (d) ephemeral : immortal

41. Thermometer : Temperature
   (a) Millimetre : Scale
   (b) Length : Breadth
   (c) Solar Energy : Sun
   (d) Cardiograph : Heart rate

42. Border : Country
   (a) Pen : Cap
   (b) Book : Cover
   (c) Handle : Shade
   (d) Frame : Picture

43. River : Ocean
   (a) Child : School
   (b) Book : Library
   (c) Lane : Road
   (d) Cloth : Body

44. Arc : Circle
   (a) Number : Count
   (b) Fraction : Percentage
   (c) Pie : Slice
   (d) Segment : Line

45. Sound : Muffled
   (a) Moisture : Humid
   (b) Colour : Faded
   (c) Despair : Anger
   (d) Odour : Pungent

46. Platform : Train
   (a) Aeroplane : Aerodrome
   (b) Hotel : Tourist
   (c) Quay : Ship
   (d) Footpath : Traveller

47. Train : Track
   (a) Water : Boat
   (b) Bullet : Barrel
   (c) Idea : Brain
   (d) Fame : Television

48. Chalk : Blackboard
   (a) Type : Point
   (b) Table : Chair
   (c) Door : Handle
   (d) Ink : Paper

49. Rectangle : Pentagon
   (a) Side : Angle
   (b) Diagonal : Perimeter
   (c) Triangle : Rectangle
   (d) Circle : Square

50. Cube : Cuboid
   (a) Oval : Sphere
   (b) Square : Cube
   (c) Sphere: Ellipsoid
   (d) Triangle : Cone

Type 3: Simple Analogy

Direction (51 to 60):

In each of the following questions, the first two words have definite relationship. Choose one word out of the given four alternatives which will show the same relationship with the third word as between the first two.

51. Artist is to painting as senator is to
   (a) Attorney   (b) Law
   (c) Politician   (d) Constituents

52. Exercise is to gym as eating is to
   (a) Food   (b) Dieting
   (c) Fitness   (d) Restaurant

53. Candid is to indirect as honest is to
   (a) Frank   (b) Wicked
   (c) Truthful   (d) Untruthful

54. Guide is to direct as reduce is to
   (a) Decrease   (b) Maintain
   (c) Increase   (d) Preserve

55. Careful is to cautious as boastful is to
    (a) Arrogant   (b) Humble
    (c) Joyful   (d) Suspicious

56. Pen is to poet as needle is to
    (a) Thread   (b) Button
    (c) Sewing   (d) Tailor

57. Secretly is to openly as silently is to
    (a) Scarcely   (b) Impolitely
    (c) Noisily   (d) Quietly

58. Pride is to lion as shoal is to
    (a) Teacher   (b) Student
    (c) Self-respect   (d) Fish

59. Yard is to inch as quart is to
    (a) Gallon   (b) Ounce
    (c) Milk   (d) Liquid

60. Cup is to coffee as bowl is to
    (a) Dish   (b) Soup
    (c) Spoon   (d) Food

Type 4: Group Analogy

Direction (61 to 70):

Each of the following questions has a group. Find out which one of the given alternatives will be another member of the group or of that class.

61. Pathology,   Cardiology,   Radiology, Ophthalmology
    (a) Biology   (b) Haematology
    (c) Zoology   (d) Geology

62. Wheat, Barley, Rice
    (a) Food   (b) Agriculture
    (c) Farm   (d) Gram

63. Lock, Shut, Fasten
    (a) Window   (b) Door
    (c) Iron   (d) Block

64. Lucknow, Patna, Bhopal, Jaipur
    (a) Shimla   (b) Mysore
    (c) Pune   (d) Indore

65. Tamilian, Gujarati, Punjabi
    (a) Aryan   (b) Dravidan

    (c) Indian   (d) Barbarian

66. Clutch, Brake, Horn
    (a) Car   (b) Scooter
    (c) Accident   (d) Steering

67. Wrestling, Karate, Boxing
    (a) Pole-vault   (b) Swimming
    (c) Judo   (d) Polo

68. Newspaper, Hoarding, Television
    (a) Press   (b) Media
    (c) Rumour   (d) Broadcast

69. Arid, Parched, Droughty
    (a) Draft   (b) Earth
    (c) Dry   (d) Cow

70. Engine, Compartment, Wheels
    (a) Motor   (b) Ship
    (c) Sea   (d) Rail-line

Non-Verbal Analogy

Direction (71 to 80):

In each of the following questions, two sets of figures are given. The first two problem figures bear a certain relationship. Based on the same relationship (analogy), select from answer figures an appropriate figure to replace the question mark in problem figures:

71.
Problem Figures

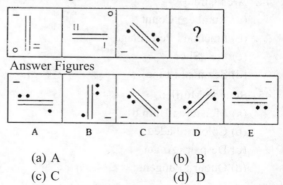

Answer Figures

    (a) A   (b) B
    (c) C   (d) D
    (e) E

72.

Problem Figures

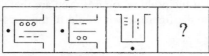

Answer Figures

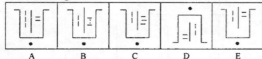

(a) A   (b) B

(c) C   (d) D

(e) E

73.

Problem Figures

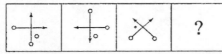

Answer Figures

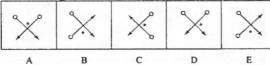

(a) A   (b) B

(c) C   (d) D

(e) E

74.

Problem Figures

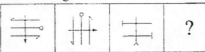

Answer Figures

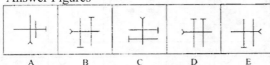

(a) A   (b) B

(c) C   (d) D

(e) E

75.

Problem Figures

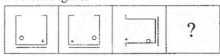

Answer Figures

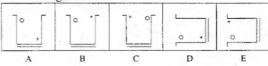

(a) A   (b) B

(c) C   (d) D

(e) E

76.

Problem Figures

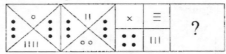

Answer Figures

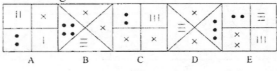

(a) A   (b) B

(c) C   (d) D

(e) E

77.

Problem Figures

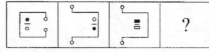

Answer Figures

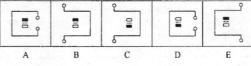

(a) A   (b) B

(c) C   (d) D

(e) E

78.

Problem Figures

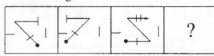

Answer Figures

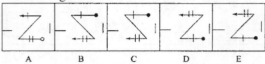

(a) A   (b) B
(c) C   (d) D
(e) E

79.

Problem Figures

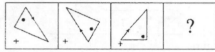

Answer Figures

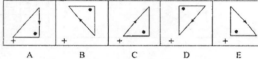

(a) A   (b) B
(c) C   (d) D
(e) E

80.

Problem Figures

Answer Figures

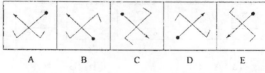

(a) A   (b) B
(c) C   (d) D
(e) E

Direction (81 to 90):

The second figure in the first unit of problem figures bears a certain relationship to the first figure.

Similarly, one of the figures in the answer figures bears the same relationship to the first figure in the second unit of the problem figures. You are therefore to locate the figure which would fit the question mark.

81.

Problem Figures

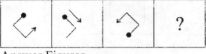

Answer Figures

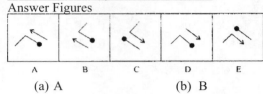

(a) A   (b) B
(c) C   (d) D
(e) E

82.

Problem Figures

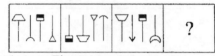

Answer Figures

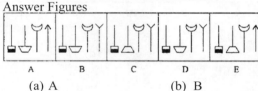

(a) A   (b) B
(c) C   (d) D
(e) E

83.

Problem Figures

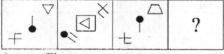

Answer Figures

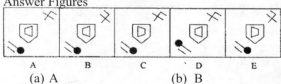

(a) A   (b) B
(c) C   (d) D
(e) E

84.

Problem Figures

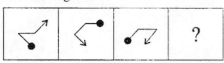

Answer Figures

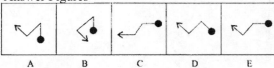

(a) A　　　　　　　(b) B
(c) C　　　　　　　(d) D
(e) E

85.

Problem Figures

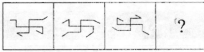

Answer Figures

(a) A　　　　　　　(b) B
(c) C　　　　　　　(d) D
(e) E

86.

Problem Figures

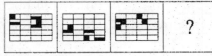

Answer Figures

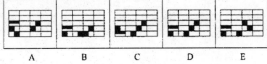

(a) A　　　　　　　(b) B
(c) C　　　　　　　(d) D
(e) E

87.

Problem Figures

Answer Figures

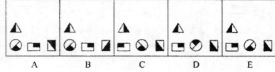

(a) A　　　　　　　(b) B
(c) C　　　　　　　(d) D
(e) E

88.

Problem Figures

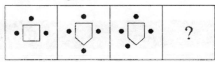

Answer Figures

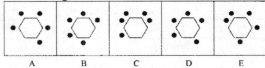

(a) A　　　　　　　(b) B
(c) C　　　　　　　(d) D
(e) E

89.

Problem Figures

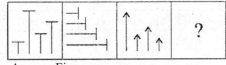

Answer Figures

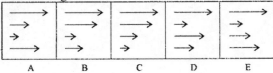

(a) A　　　　　　　(b) B
(c) C　　　　　　　(d) D
(e) E

90.

Problem Figures

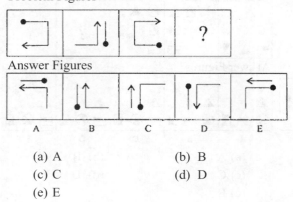

Answer Figures

(a) A
(b) B
(c) C
(d) D
(e) E

Hints and Solutions

1. **(b)**
   As Physician does the treatment, similarly Judge delivers the judgement.

2. **(c)**
   As effect of Ice is coldness, similarly the effect of Earth is gravitation.

3. **(c)**
   As the result of Race is Fatigue, similarly the result of Fast is Hunger.

4. **(c)**
   As opposite meaning of peace is chaos, similarly opposite meaning of creation is destruction.

5. **(d)**
   As Tiger is found in Forest, similarly Otter is found in the water.

6. **(c)**
   As magnet has poles, similarly battery has terminals.

7. **(d)**
   A Priest wears cassock while Graduate wears gown.

8. **(a)**
   As President is the nominal head of a country, similarly Governor is the nominal head of a State.

9. **(d)**
   As Cloth is made in a mill, similarly Newspaper is printed in press.

10. **(c)**
    As North-West is $135°$ clockwise from South, in the same way North-East is $135°$ clockwise from the West.

11. **(a)**
    As Tree is found in forest, similarly Grass is found in lawn.

12. **(d)**
    As Students read in college, similarly Patients are treated in hospital.

13. **(d)**
    As Chairman is the highest authority in a conference, similarly Editor is in newspaper.

14. **(c)**
    As Microphone makes sound louder, similarly Microscope makes the object magnified.

15. **(c)**
    As on melting, liquid is formed, similarly on freezing solid is formed.

16. **(c)**
    As, 123   132
    Similarly, 235   253
    The middle digit becomes power.

17. **(d)**
    As, $14 = (2 × 9 − 4)$
    Similarly, $26 = (2 × 15 − 4)$
    $\therefore ? = 15$

18. **(c)**
    As positions of M and N in Eq. alphabets are 13 and 14 respectively, similarly F and R hold 6 and 18 positions respectively.

19. **(b)**
    As, $16:56 = (2/7)$
    Similarly, $32:112 :(2/7)$

20. **(a)**
    As, $(4)^2 + 3 = 19$
    Similarly, $(7)^2 + 3 = 52$

21. **(c)**
    As $24 : 60 = (2/5)$
    Similarly, $(120/300) = (2/5)$

22. **(a)**
    As $335 − 216 = 119$
    Similarly, $987 − X = 119$
    Therefore, $X = 987 − 119 = 868$

23. **(b)**
    As, 24 $2 × 4 = 8$
    Similarly, 32 $3 × 2 = 6$

24. **(a)**
    Here, $9 = (3)^2$
    $8 = (3 − 1)^3$
    and $16 = (4)^2$
    $? = (4 − 1)^3 = 27$

25. **(a)**

In Eq. alphabets positions of K and T are 11 and 20 respectively.

Similarly positions of J and R are 10 and 18.

26. **(d)**

An aerie is where an eagle lives; a house is where a person lives.

27. **(b)**

Being erudite is a trait of a professor; being imaginative is a trait of an inventor.

28. **(a)**

The deltoid is a muscle; the radius is a bone.

29. **(a)**

Jaundice is an indication of a liver problem; rash is an indication of a skin problem.

30. **(a)**

A conviction results in incarceration; a reduction results in diminution.

31. **(d)**

Dependable and capricious are antonyms; capable and inept are antonyms.

32. **(d)**

A metaphor is a symbol; an analogy is a comparison.

33. **(c)**

Obsession is a greater degree of interest; fantasy is a greater degree of dream.

34. **(d)**

A conductor leads an orchestra; a skipper leads a crew.

35. **(a)**

A palm (tree) has fronds; a porcupine has quills.

36. **(c)**

A cacophony is an unpleasant sound; a stench is an unpleasant smell.

37. **(d)**

Umbrage and offense are synonyms; elation and jubilance are synonyms.

38. **(d)**

A dirge is a song used at a funeral; a jingle is a song used in commercial.

39. **(d)**

To be phobic is to be extremely fearful; to be asinine is to be extremely silly.

40. **(d)**

Feral and tame are antonyms; ephemeral and immortal are antonyms.

41. **(d)**

As temperature is measured by a thermometer, in the same way heart rate is measured by cardiograph.

42. **(d)**

First is the boundary of the second.

43. **(c)**

As River joints to Ocean, similarly Lane joints to Road.

44. **(d)**

As Arc is a part of Circle, similarly segment is a part of line.

45. **(b)**

Second is the process of gradual disappearance of the first.

46. **(c)**

First is the place where second stops.

47. **(b)**

As Train is guided by the track, similarly Bullet is guided by the barrel.

48. **(d)**

As chalk is used to write on the blackboard, similarly ink is used to write on the paper.

49. **(c)**

Second one had one more side than the first.

50. **(c)**

Second is elongated form of the first.

51. **(b)**

An artist makes paintings; a senator makes laws. The answer is not choice (a) because an attorney does not make laws and a senator is not an attorney. Choice c is incorrect because a senator is not a politician. A constituent (choice d) is also incorrect because a senator serves his or her constituents.

52. **(d)**

A gym is a place where people exercise. A restaurant is a place where people eat. Food (choice a) is not the answer because it is something people eat, not a place or location where they eat. The answer is not choice b or c because neither represents a place where people eat.

53. **(d)**

Candid and indirect refer to opposite traits. Honest and untruthful refer to opposite traits. The answer is not choice (a) because frank means the same thing as candid. Wicked (choice b) is incorrect because even though it refers to a negative trait, it does not mean the opposite of honest. (Choice c) is incorrect because truthful and honest mean the same thing.

54. **(a)**

Guide and direct are synonyms, and reduce and decrease are synonyms. The answer is not choice b or d because neither means the same as reduce. (Choice c) is incorrect because increase is the opposite of reduce.

55. **(a)**

Careful and cautious are synonyms (they mean the same thing). Boastful and arrogant are also synonyms. The answer is not (choice b) because humble means the opposite of boastful. The answer is not choice c or d because neither means the same as boastful.

56. **(d)**

A pen is a tool used by a poet. A needle is a tool used by a tailor. The answer is not choice a, b, or c because none is a person and therefore cannot complete the analogy.

57. **(c)**

Secretly is the opposite of openly, and silently is the opposite of noisily. Choices a and b are clearly not the opposites of silently. (Choice d) means the same thing as silently.

58. **(d)**

A group of lions is called a pride. A group of fish swim in a shoal. Teacher (choice a) and student (choice b) refer to another meaning of the word school. The answer is not (choice c) because self-respect has no obvious relationship to this particular meaning of school.

59. **(b)**

A yard is a larger measure than an inch (a yard contains 36 inches). A quart is a larger measure than an ounce (a quart contains 32 ounces). Gallon (choice a) is incorrect because it is larger than a quart. Choices c and d are incorrect because they are not units of measurement.

60. **(b)**

Coffee goes into a cup and soup goes into a bowl. Choices a and c are incorrect because they are other utensils. The answer is not choice d because the word food is too general.

61. **(b)**

As the all terms given in the question are medical terms and Haematology is also a medical term.

62. **(d)**

All the terms given in the question are cereals and gram is also one of the cereals.

63. **(d)**

The synonym of Lock, Shut and Fasten is Block.

64. **(a)**

All the cities given in the question are state capitals, similarly Shimla is also a capital.

65. **(c)**

All these words represent the inhabitants of India.

66. **(d)**

All these are parts of a vehicle.

67. **(c)**

These are all defensive games.

68. **(d)**

All these are used for broadcast.

69. **(c)**

The synonym of arid, parched and droughty is dry.

70. **(d)**

All these are related to train.

71. **(d)**

As per pattern minus sign should be in right corner, parallel lines rotate through 90° and position of dots gets inverted.

72. **(e)**

The inner figures are inverted. The number of lines and dots decrease by one.

73. **(d)**

Two lines are get inverted. The position of dots is changed in order.

74. **(b)**

The figure gets rotated through 90° ACW.

75. **(d)**

The inner images are inverted. + sign changes to x.

76. **(e)**

First and fourth quadrants are same. Second and third quadrants are inverted with two dots decreased and one cross increased respectively.

77. **(d)**

The figure rotates through 180° and outer side should be inside.

78. **(d)**

The figure gets rotated with 180° only, and we get the required image.

79. **(d)**

The figure gets rotated with 180°. The arrow placed on hypotenuse should be in downward direction.

80. **(d)**

As per pattern in final image the arrow should be in right corner and in upward direction.

81. **(b)**

Black dot should be in right corner with opposite direction of arrow and arrow should be under the black dot.

82. **(d)**

Third image should be in first place and gets inverted. First image should be in second place and gets inverted. Second image should be in fourth place and only outer part be inverted. We have to follow same pattern with fourth image.

83. **(c)**

As per pattern trapezium should be in middle inside the pentagon with ninety degree rotation. Similar pattern will be followed with rest of the image.

84. **(a)**

Arrow should be in right corner with upward direction. Line with black dot rotates through 45° ACW.

85. **(b)**

All the outer parts gets inside and inner part gets outside.

86. **(d)**

Shifting the shaded portion in opposite direction, we get the required image.

87. **(d)**

All the figures get inverted.

88. **(d)**

The number of dots is one less than the number of sides.

89. **(b)**

The number of positions of arrow are changed in order.

90. **(d)**

As per pattern the image includes arrow rotated through 90° and then inverts. The image with black dot should be in opposite direction with arrow.

3   Series Completion

In Series Completion, a series of numbers or alphabet letters or combination of both numbers and letters is given. Each of the number or letter is called as term of the series. The terms of the series follow a particular pattern through the series. The candidate has to analyse the series and find out the certain pattern which is applied for whole of the series. Basically series completion is based on numbers. Each succeeding term of the series may be obtained by adding, subtracting multiplying or dividing by some number, which is same for whole of the series. Sometimes the alternate terms of the series obeys the certain pattern.

So, we have to analyse the terms of the series and then find out the missing term or wrong term in the given series. The candidate should study the given series, identify the pattern followed in the series and either complete the given series with most suitable alternative or find the wrong in the given series.

Example 1:   53, 65, 77, 89, ?

     Solution: 53   65   77   89   101

                 +12   +12   +12   +12

                 The next number = 101.

Example 2:   0, 3, 8, 15, 24, 35, 48, 63, ?

     Solution: 0   3   8   15   24   35   48   63   80

              $1^2 - 1$ $2^2 - 1$ $3^2 - 1$ $4^2 - 1$ $5^2 - 1$ $6^2 - 1$ $7^2 - 1$ $8^2 - 1$ $9^2 - 1$

              $\therefore$ Next number = 80.

Example 3:   −17, −7, 3, 13, 23, 33, ?

     Solution: −17 + 10 = −7

              −7 + 10 = 3

              3 + 10 = 13

              13 + 10 = 23

              $\therefore$ Next number = 33 + 10 = 43.

Example 4:   7, 14, 28, 56, 112, 224, ?

     Solution: 7 × 2 = 14

              14 × 2 = 28

              $\therefore$ Next term = 224 × 2 = 448.

Example 5:   47, 52, 49, 54, 51, 56, 53, ?

     Solution: 47   52   49   54   51   56   53   58

               +5   −3   +5   −3   +5   −3   +5

              $\therefore$? = 58

Example 6: 331, 553, 775, 997, ?

Solution: 331 + 222 = 553

553 + 222 = 775

∴ Next term = 997 + 222 = 1219.

Example 7: 17, 85, 340, 1020, 2040, ?

Solution: 17 × 5 = 85

85 × 4 = 340

340 × 3 = 1020

1020 × 2 = 2040

Multiple Choice Questions

1. 67, 74, 81, 88, 95, ?
   (a) 101   (b) 102
   (c) 103   (d) 104

2. 109, 101, 94, 88, 83, ?
   (a) 78   (b) 79
   (c) 80   (d) 81

3. 9, 25, 49, 81, 121, ?
   (a) 141   (b) 144
   (c) 161   (d) 169

4. 3, 8, 15, 24, 35, 48, ?
   (a) 61   (b) 62
   (c) 63   (d) 64

5. 6, 12, 24, 48, 96, 192, ?
   (a) 384   (b) 386
   (c) 388   (d) 392

6. 4, 3, 4, 9, 32, 155, ?
   (a) 924   (b) 926
   (c) 928   (d) 932

7. 85, 88, 91, 94, 97, 100, 103, 106, ?
   (a) 109   (b) 110
   (c) 111   (d) 112

8. 5, 10, 40, 80, 320, 640, ?
   (a) 2520   (b) 2540
   (c) 2560   (d) 2580

9. 1, 5, 9, 17, 25, 37, 49, ?
   (a) 64   (b) 63
   (c) 65   (d) 67

10. 6, 15, 35, 77, 143, ?
    (a) 221   (b) 223
    (c) 225   (d) 227

11. 16, 22, 30, 40, 52, 66, 82, ?
    (a) 100   (b) 98
    (c) 102   (d) 104

12. 225, 205, 180, 150, 115, ?
    (a) 55   (b) 65
    (c) 75   (d) 85

13. 10, 14, 28, 32, 64, 68, ?
    (a) 136   (b) 72
    (c) 126   (d) 82

14. 3, 4, 10, 33, 136, ?
    (a) 682   (b) 684
    (c) 685   (d) 687'

15. 1326, 2436, 3546, 4656, ?
    (a) 5760   (b) 5766
    (c) 5667   (d) 5768

16. 598, 505, 412, 319, 226, ?
    (a) 131   (b) 132
    (c) 133   (d) 134

17. 702, 773, 844, 915, 986, ?
    (a) 1052   (b) 1053
    (c) 1056   (d) 1057

18. 15, 45,42, 126, 123, 369, 366, ?
    (a) 1094   (b) 1095
    (c) 1096   (d) 1098

19. 27, 56, 114, 230, 462, 926, ?
    (a) 1852   (b) 1854
    (c) 1848   (d) 1856

20. 2, 21, 154, 1085, 7602, ?
    (a) 53214   (b) 53216
    (c) 53221   (d) 53223

21. 377, 318, 259, 200, 141, ?
    (a) 92   (b) 82
    (c) 72   (d) 76

22. 137, 248, 359, 470, 581, 692, ?
    (a) 801   (b) 802
    (c) 803   (d) None of these

23. 13, 65, 325, 1625, 8125, ?
    (a) 40625   (b) 41625
    (c) 40675   (d) 41675

Answer Key

1. (b)	2. (b)	3. (d)	4. (c)	5. (a)	6. (a)	7. (a)	8. (c)	9. (c)	10 (a)
11. (a)	12. (c)	13. (a)	14. (c)	15. (b)	16. (c)	17. (d)	18. (d)	19. (b)	20. (c)
21. (b)	22. (c)	23. (a)							

Hints _and_ Solutions

1. **(b)** The given series is

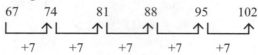

2. **(b)** The given series is

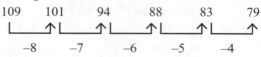

3. **(d)** The given series is

$$
\begin{array}{cccccc}
9 & 25 & 49 & 81 & 121 & 169 \\
\uparrow & \uparrow & \uparrow & \uparrow & \uparrow & \uparrow \\
3^2 & 5^2 & 7^2 & 9^2 & 11^2 & 13^2
\end{array}
$$

4. **(c)** The given series is

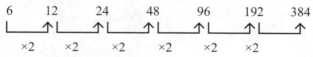

$$(2^2-1) \quad (3^2-1) \quad (4^2-1) \quad (5^2-1) \quad (6^2-1) \quad (7^2-1) \quad (8^2-1) \quad (9^2-1)$$

5. **(a)** The given series is

$$
\begin{array}{ccccccc}
6 & 12 & 24 & 48 & 96 & 192 & 384
\end{array}
$$

$$\times 2 \quad \times 2 \quad \times 2 \quad \times 2 \quad \times 2 \quad \times 2$$

6. **(a)** The given series is

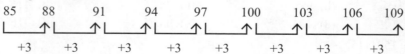

$$\times 1-1 \quad \times 2-2 \quad \times 3-3 \quad \times 4-4 \quad \times 5-5 \quad \times 6-6$$

7. **(a)** The given series is

$$
\begin{array}{ccccccccc}
85 & 88 & 91 & 94 & 97 & 100 & 103 & 106 & 109
\end{array}
$$

$$+3 \quad +3 \quad +3 \quad +3 \quad +3 \quad +3 \quad +3 \quad +3$$

8. **(c)** The given series is

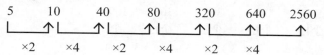

5　　10　　40　　80　　320　　640　　2560

×2　×4　×2　×4　×2　×4

9. **(c)** The given series is

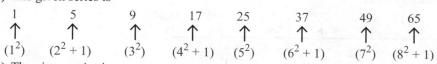

1　　5　　9　　17　　25　　37　　49　　65

(1^2)　$(2^2 + 1)$　(3^2)　$(4^2 + 1)$　(5^2)　$(6^2 + 1)$　(7^2)　$(8^2 + 1)$

10. **(a)** The given series is

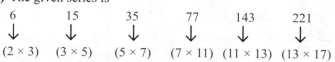

6　　15　　35　　77　　143　　221

(2×3)　(3×5)　(5×7)　(7×11)　(11×13)　(13×17)

11. **(a)** The given series is

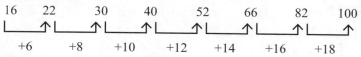

16　22　　30　　40　　52　　66　　82　　100

+6　+8　+10　+12　+14　+16　+18

12. **(c)** The given series is

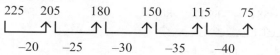

225　205　　180　　150　　115　　75

−20　−25　−30　−35　−40

13. **(a)** The given series is

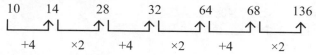

10　14　　28　　32　　64　　68　　136

+4　×2　+4　×2　+4　×2

14. **(c)** The given series is

3　4　　10　　33　　136　　685

×1 + 1　×2 + 2　×3 + 3　×4 + 4　×5 + 5

15. **(b)** The given series is

1326　2436　3546　4656　5766

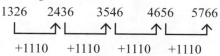

+1110　+1110　+1110　+1110

16. **(c)** The given series is

598　505　　412　　319　　226　　133

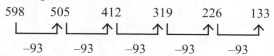

−93　−93　−93　−93　−93

17. **(d)** The given series is

702　773　　844　　915　　986　　1057

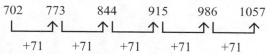

+71　+71　+71　+71　+71

18. **(d)** The given series is

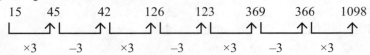

19. **(b)** The given series is

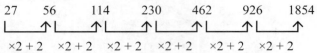

20. **(c)** The given series is

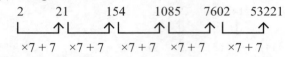

21. **(b)** The given series is

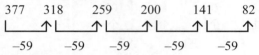

22. **(c)** The given series is

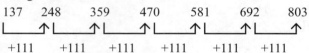

23. **(a)** The given series is

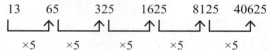

In the questions based on odd one out a group of words are given, in which one word is completely different from the other words. Some words have a common quality and have same characteristics. In this type of problems, generally there are fours words or numbers or pair of words in which three are same in some particular manner but one word, number or pair of words is different from the other three.

Example: In a group of words three words belong to vegetables and one word is a type of fruit, then the word which is fruit is odd from the others.

Find the Odd One Out:

    (a) Coward : Brave   (b) Beginning : End

    (c) White : Dirty   (c) Easy : Difficult

In the above pairs of words option (c) is odd, as all others are antonyms of each other.

Find the Odd One Out :

    (a) 121   (b) 169

    (c) 256   (d) 145

In these numbers (a) (b) (c) are perfect squares but (d) is not a perfect square. So, 145 is odd.

Thus, 'Odd one out' means to assort items of a given group on the basis of a certain common property they have possess and then spot the stranger or 'odd one out' .

Examples 1: Choose the odd one out from the following:

    (a) Tiger   (b) Horse

    (c) Lion   (d) Giraffe

    Solution: (b) All except Horse, are wild animals, while Horse can be domesticated.

Examples 2:

    (a) January   (b) May

    (c) November   (d) July

    Solution: (c) All except November are months having 31 days, while November has 30 days.

Examples 3:

    (a) Sword   (b) Gun

    (c) Rifle   (d) Cannon

    Solution: (a) All except Sword are fire arms, and can be used from a distance.

Examples 4:

    (a) Mercury   (b) Petrol

    (c) Kerosene   (d) Acetone

    Solution: (a) Mercury is the only metal in the group.

Examples 5:

    (a) Soda water   (b) Beer

    (c) Cold drink   (d) Milk

Solution: (d) All except milk are artificially prepared drinks.

Examples 6:

    (a) Day   (b) Calendar

    (c) Month   (d) Fortnight

Solution: (b) All others are parts of a calendar.

Examples 7:

    (a) Rhea   (b) Lamprey

    (c) Salmon   (d) Trout

Solution: (a) All except Rhea are kinds of fishes.

Examples 8:

    (a) Bars   (b) Lagoons

    (c) Beaches   (d) Moraines

Solution: (d) All except Moraines are structures formed by the sea, while moraines are formed by glaciers.

Examples 9:

    (a) Accumulate   (b) Congregate

    (c) Aggregate   (d) Disperse

Solution: (d) All except Disperse are synonyms of 'collect'.

Examples 10:

    (a) Insulin   (b) Iodine

    (c) Adrenaline   (d) Thyroxine

Solution: (b) All except Iodine are hormones.

Multiple Choice Questions

Direction : Choose the odd one out from the following.

1.
   (a) History   (b) Physics
   (c) Civics   (d) Geography

2.
   (a) Mosque   (b) Temple
   (c) Mantery   (d) Church

3.
   (a) Operating system   (b) Hard disk
   (c) Printer   (d) Pendrive

4.
   (a) Ruby   (b) Marble
   (c) Sapphire   (d) Diamond

5.
   (a) Peel   (b) Fry
   (c) Roast   (d) Bake

6.
   (a) Silicon   (b) Potassium
   (c) Gallium   (d) Germanium

7.
   (a) Kiwi   (b) Emu
   (c) Eagle   (d) Penguiv

8.
   (a) Tomato   (b) Carrot
   (c) Brinjal   (d) Gourd

9.
   (a) India   (b) Japan
   (c) Sri Lanka   (d) Malagasy

10.
   (a) Spectacles   (b) Goggles
   (c) Microphone (d) Telescope

11.
   (a) Hammer   (b) Dagger
   (c) Sword   (d) Knife

12.
   (a) Trunk   (b) Tree
   (c) Leaf   (d) Flower

13.
   (a) Dog   (b) Horse
   (c) Fox   (d) Cat

14.
   (a) Cap   (b) Helmet
   (c) Veil   (d) Hat

15.
   (a) Write   (b) Read
   (c) Learn   (d) Knowledge

16.
   (a) Radio   (b) X-ray
   (c) Computer   (d) Television

17.
   (a) Earth   (b) Venus
   (c) Saturn   (d) Mercury

18.
   (a) Cabbage   (b) Cauliflower
   (c) Radish   (d) Lady finger

19.
   (a) Delicious   (b) Sour
   (c) Bitter   (d) Sweet

20.
   (a) Cotton   (b) Nylon
   (c) Silk   (d) Wool

21.
   (a) Nail   (b) Feather
   (c) Fir   (d) Trunk

22.
   (a) Arhar   (b) Jower
   (c) Moong   (d) Gram

23.
   (a) Blood   (b) Bones
   (c) Muscles   (d) Tendons

24.
   (a) Cool   (b) Warm
   (c) Hot   (d) Humid

25.
  (a) Leh   (b) Aizwal
  (c) Shimla   (d) Panaji

26.
  (a) Yak   (b) Leopard
  (c) Silver fox (d) Reindeep

27.
  (a) Pineapple (b) Malta
  (c) Banana   (d) Lemon

28.
  (a) Faraday   (b) Newton
  (c) Marconi   (d) Beethovan

29.
  (a) Indigo   (b) Green
  (c) Pink   (d) Yellow

30.
  (a) Whale   (b) Cod
  (c) Starfish   (d) Shark

31.
  (a) Father   (b) Cousin
  (c) Uncle   (d) Aunt

32.
  (a) Cancel   (b) Repeal
  (c) Change   (d) Revoke

33.
  (a) Mamba   (b) Cobra
  (c) Viper   (d) Python

34.
  (a) Medium   (b) Average
  (c) Terrible   (d) Mediocre

35.
  (a) Yeast   (b) Mould
  (c) Smut   (d) Mushroom

36.
  (a) Wood   (b) Stone
  (c) Cork   (d) Paper

37.
  (a) Beam   (b) Wall
  (c) Roof   (d) House

38.
  (a) Cry   (b) Sad
  (c) Laugh   (d) Weep

39.
  (a) Nymph   (b) Caterpillar
  (c) Pupa   (d) Larva

40.
  (a) Oil   (b) Glue
  (c) Paste   (d) Cement

Answer Key

1. (b)	2. (c)	3. (a)	4. (b)	5. (a)	6. (b)	7. (c)	8. (b)	9. (a)	10 (c)
11. (a)	12. (b)	13. (c)	14. (c)	15. (d)	16. (b)	17. (a)	18. (d)	19. (a)	20. (b)
21. (c)	22.(b)	23. (c)	24. (a)	25. (a)	26. (b)	27. (c)	28. (d)	29. (c)	30. (a)
31. (b)	32. (c)	33. (d)	34. (c)	35. (c)	36. (b)	37. (d)	38. (b)	39. (a)	40. (a)

Hints *and* Solutions

4. **(b)**
   All except marble are precious stones.

5. **(a)**
   All except peel are different form of cooking.

6. **(b)**
   All except potassium are metal used in semiconductor devices.

7. **(c)**
   All except Eagle are flightless birds.

9. **(a)**
   All except India are islands, while India is a Peninsula.

11. **(a)**
   All except Hammer are sharp edged and have a cutting action.

12. **(b)**
   All others are parts of tree.

17. **(a)**
   All except Earth denote Roman or Greek Gods.

20. **(b)**
   All except Nylon are natural fibres, while nylon is a synthetic fibre.

25. **(a)**
   All except Leh are capitals of Indian states, while Leh is a hill station.

26. **(b)**
   All except Leopard are found in Polar regions.

28. **(d)**
   All except Beethovan were Scientists, while Beethovan was a musician.

29. **(c)**
   All except Pink are the colours seen in a rainbow.

33. **(d)**
   All except Python are venomous snakes.

34. **(c)**
   All except Terrible are synonyms.

35. **(c)**
   All except Smut are forms of fungi.

36. **(b)**
   All except stone are obtained directly or indirectly from trees.

37. **(d)**
   All others are parts of house.

39. **(a)**
   All except Nymph are stages in the life cycle of a butterfly, while nymph is a young cockroack.

5 Coding – Decoding

Coding is a method of transmitting a message between the sender and receiver without a third person knowing it. A code is nothing but a system of signals. There are various types of coding namely letter coding, direct letter coding, number and symbol, coding, substitution, deciphering message word codes etc.

In letter coding, the letters in a word are replaced by certain words according to a particular rule to form its code. The candidate is required to detect the coding pattern and answer the question according to the pattern.

In direct letter coding particular, letters are made code for particular letters without any set patterns. In direct coding, the code letters occur in the same sequence as the corresponding letters occur in the words.

In number/symbol coding, numerical code values are assigned in a word or alphabetical code. Letters are assigned to the numbers, then the candidate is required to analyse the rule as per the question.

Now, we will learn different types of Coding and Decoding methods.

Letter Coding

The letters in a word are replaced by certain other letters according to a specific rule to form its code.

Example 1: If BOMBAY is written as MYMYMY, how will TAMILNADU be written in that code?

    (a) MNUMNUMNU

    (b) IATIATIAT

    (c) ALDALDALD

    (d) TIATIATIA

Solution: (a)

The letters at the third and sixth places are repeated thrice to code BOMBAY as MYMYMY. Similarly, the letters at the third, sixth and ninth places are repeated thrice to code TAMILNADU as MNUMNUMNU.

Example 2: In a certain code language, THANKS is written as SKNTHA. HOW is STUPID written in that code language?

    (a) DIPUTS

    (b) DISPUT

    (c) DIPUST

    (d) DPISTU

Solution: (d)

The code is formed by just writing the last three letters of the word in a reverse order, followed by the first three letters in the same order. So, the code for STUPID should be DIPSTU.

Direct Letter Coding

Letters were assigned codes according to a set pattern or rule concerning the movement or reordering of letters and one needs to detect this hidden rule to decode a message.

Such type of coding is called direct – coding. The code letters occurs in the same sequence as the corresponding letters occur in the words.

Example 3: If TEACHER is coded as LMKJMMP, then how will HEART be coded?

    (a) NMKPL   (b) NPKML
    (c) MMPKL   (d) MMAPL

Solution: (a)

    Letter : T   E   A   C   H   R
    Code :   L   M   K   J   N   P

    The code for HEART is NMKPL.

Number/Symbol Coding

Numerical code values are assigned to a word or alphabetical code letters are assigned to the numbers.

Letters and numbers are correlated to each other in no other way except in relation to the position of the letters in the English alphabet.

Example 4: If MOBILITY is coded as 46293927, then EXAMINATION is coded as.

    (a) 67250623076
    (b) 57159413955
    (c) 56149512965
    (d) 45038401

Solution: (c)

Let $A = 1$, $B = 2$, $C = 3$, ……., $X = 24$, $Y = 25$, $Z = 26$.
$M = 13 = 1 + 3 = 4$; $O = 15 = 1 + 5 = 6$; $B = 2$; $I = 9$; $L = 12 = 1 + 2 = 3$
$T = 20 = 2 + 0 = 2$; $Y = 25 = 2 + 5 = 7$.
So, MOBILITY = 46293927
$X = 24 = 2 + 4 = 6$; $N = 14 = 1 + 4 = 5$.
So, EXAMINATION = 56149512965.

Example 5: If REASON is coded as 5 and BELIEVED as 7, then what is the code for GOVERNMENT?

    (a) 10   (b) 9
    (c) 8   (d) 6

Solution: (b)

Clearly, each word is coded by the numeral which is 1 less than the number of letters in the word.

Substitution

In this type of question, some particular words are assigned certain substituted names.

Example 6: If 'rain' is 'water', 'water' is 'road', 'road' is 'cloud', 'cloud' is 'sky', 'sky' is 'sea' and 'sea' is path where do aeroplanes fly?

    (a) Sea   (b) Water
    (c) Cloud   (d) Road

Solution: (a)

Multiple Choice Questions

1. If TRUTH is coded as SUQSTVSUGI, then the code for FALSE will be
   - (a) FGZBKNRTDF
   - (b) EGZBKMRDE
   - (c) EGZKMRTDF
   - (d) EGZBKMRTDF

2. In a certain code, INACTIVE is written as VITCANIE. How is COMPUTER written in the same code?
   - (a) UTEPMOCR
   - (b) MOCPETUR
   - (c) ETUPMOCR
   - (d) PMOCRETU

3. In a certain code, COVALENT, is written as BWPDUOFM and FORM is written as PGNS. How will SILVER be written in that code?
   - (a) MJTSFW
   - (b) MJTWFS
   - (c) KHRSFW
   - (d) None of these

4. In a certain code, VISHWANATHAN is written as NAAWTHHSANIV. How is KARUMAKARANA written in that code?
   - (a) KAAMRAURMAAK
   - (b) NKKRAMKRAUK
   - (c) RURNKAAUNAK
   - (d) AKNUARRAANKA

5. In a certain code, MOTHER is written as ONHURF. How will ANSWER be written in that code?
   - (a) NBWRRF
   - (b) MAVSPE
   - (c) NBWTRF
   - (d) NBXSSE

6. In a certain code, the words COME AT ONCE, were written as XLNVZGLMXV. In the same code, which of the following would code OK?
   - (a) LP
   - (b) KM
   - (c) LM
   - (d) KL

7. In a certain code, RAIL is written as KCTN and SPEAK is written as CGRUM. How will AVOID be written in that code?
   - (a) FKQXC
   - (b) KQVCB
   - (c) KQXCF
   - (d) KRXCF

8. If CONTRIBUTE is written as ETBUIRNTOC, then which letter will be in the sixth place when counted from the left it POPULARISE is written in the same way?
   - (a) L
   - (b) A
   - (c) R
   - (d) I

9. If in a certain code, GRASP is coded as BMVMK, which word would be coded as CRANE?
   - (a) BQZMD
   - (b) HWFSJ
   - (c) GVERJ
   - (d) XMVIZ

10. If NARGRUED is the code for GRANDEUR, which word is coded as SERPEVRE?
    - (a) PRESEVER
    - (b) PERSERVE
    - (c) PERSEVER
    - (d) PRESERVE

11. If CONCEPT is written as unmulqr and FRIEND is written as ysglmt, then how is PREDICT written in that code?
    - (a) qsltgur
    - (b) qgmnltr
    - (c) slmgtur
    - (d) USXgmnl

12. In a certain code, FIRE is written as QHOE and MOVE as ZMWE. Following the same rule of coding what should be the code for the word OVER?
    - (a) MWZO
    - (b) MWED
    - (c) MWEO
    - (d) MWOE

13. If WORK is coded as 4 – 12 – 9 – 16, then how will you code WOMAN?
    - (a) 23 – 12 – 26 – 14 – 13
    - (b) 4 – 12 – 14 – 26 – 13
    - (c) 4 – 26 – 14 – 13 – 12
    - (d) 23 – 15 – 13 – 1 – 14

14. If GO = 32, SHE = 49, then SOME will be equal to
    - (a) 64
    - (b) 62
    - (c) 56
    - (d) 58

15. If ZIP = 198 and ZAP = 246, then how will you code VIP ?
    - (a) 888
    - (b) 990
    - (c) 222
    - (d) 174

16. If MASTER is coded as $\overline{411259}$, then POWDER will be coded as.
    - (a) $\overline{765549}$
    - (b) $\overline{765459}$
    - (c) $\overline{765439}$
    - (d) $\overline{765439}$

17. In a certain code, BRAIN is written as * % ÷ # × and TIER is written as $ # + %. How is RENT written in that code?
    - (a) % × # $
    - (b) % # × $
    - (c) + × % $
    - (d) % + × $

18. If DELHI is coded as 73541 and CALCUTTA as 82589662, how can CALICUT be coded?
    - (a) 8251896
    - (b) 8543691
    - (c) 5978213
    - (d) 5279431

19. If NOIDA is written as 39658, how will INDIA be written?
    - (a) 36568
    - (b) 65368
    - (c) 63568
    - (d) 63569

20. If ENGLAND is written as 1234526 and FRANCE is written as 785291, how is GREECE coded?
    - (a) 835545
    - (b) 381191
    - (c) 832252
    - (d) 381171

21. If REQUEST is written as S2R52TU, then how will ACID be written?
    - (a) ID3E
    - (b) IC94
    - (c) B3J4
    - (d) 1394

22. In a certain code, DESK is written as #. 52, RIDE is written as % 7# . how is RISK written in that code?
    - (a) % 7 $ #
    - (b) % 752
    - (c) % 7 # 2
    - (d) % 725

23. In a certain code, EAT is written as 318 and CHAIR is written as 24156. What will TEACHER be written as?
    - (a) 8313426
    - (b) 8321436
    - (c) 8312346
    - (d) 8312436

24. In a certain code, DEAF is written as 3587 and FILE is written as 7465. How is IDEAL written in that code?
    - (a) 63548
    - (b) 43568
    - (c) 43586
    - (d) 48536

25. If DRIVER = 12, PEDESTRIAN = 20, ACCIDENT = 16, then CAR = ?
    - (a) 6
    - (b) 8
    - (c) 10
    - (d) 3

26. If 'Oranges' are 'apples', 'bananas' are 'apricots', 'apples' are 'chillies', 'apricots' are 'oranges' and chillies are 'bananas', then which of the following are green in colour?
    - (a) Chillies
    - (b) Oranges
    - (c) Apples
    - (d) Bananas

27. If 'sky' is 'star', 'star' is 'cloud', 'cloud' is earth, 'earth' is 'tree' and 'tree' is 'book', then where do the birds fly?
    - (a) Sky
    - (b) Cloud
    - (c) Star
    - (d) None of these

28. If 'blue' means 'green', 'green' means 'white', 'white' means 'yellow' means 'black', 'black' means 'red' and 'red' means 'brown', then what is the colour of milk?
    - (a) Green
    - (b) Yellow
    - (c) Blue
    - (d) Black

29. If 'eraser' is called 'box', 'box' is called 'pencil', 'pencil' is called 'sharpener' and 'sharpener' is called 'bag', what will a child write with?
    - (a) Box
    - (b) Sharpener
    - (c) Bag
    - (d) Pencil

30. If 'dust' is called 'air', 'air' is called 'fire', 'fire' is called 'water', 'water' is called 'colour', 'colour' is called 'rain' and 'rain' is called 'dust', then where do fish live?
    - (a) Dust
    - (b) Water
    - (c) Colour
    - (d) Fire

1. (d)	2. (c)	3. (a)	4. (a)	5. (c)	6. (a)	7. (c)	8. (a)	9. (b)	10 (d)
11. (a)	12. (c)	13. (b)	14. (c)	15. (c)	16. (b)	17. (d)	18. (a)	19. (c)	20. (b)
21. (a)	22. (b)	23. (d)	24. (b)	25. (a)	26. (d)	27. (c)	28. (a)	29. (b)	30. (c)

Hints *and* Solutions

1. **(d)**

   Each letter of the word 'TRUTH' is replaced by a set of two letters – one preceding it and the other following it – in the code. Thus, T is replaced by SU, R is replaced by QS and so on.

2. **(c)**

   All the letters of the word, except the last letter, are written in a reverse order to obtain the code.

3. **(a)** Here,

   $$\text{SILVER} \to \text{SIL/VER} \xrightarrow{\text{Reversing}} \text{LIS/REV}$$
   $$\xrightarrow{+1} \text{MJT/SFW}$$

4. **(a)**

   Divide the given word into six sets of two letters each and label these sets from 1 to 6. Then the code contains these sets in the order 4, 3, 5, 2, 6, 1 with the letters of sets 3, 2, 1 written in a reverse order. Thus, we have:

   $$\frac{\text{VI}}{1} \; \frac{\text{SH}}{2} \; \frac{\text{WA}}{3} \; \frac{\text{NA}}{4} \; \frac{\text{TH}}{5} \; \frac{\text{AM}}{6} \to$$

   $$\frac{\text{NA}}{4} \; \frac{\text{AW}}{3} \; \frac{\text{TH}}{5} \; \frac{\text{HS}}{2} \; \frac{\text{AM}}{6} \; \frac{\text{IV}}{1}$$

5. **(c)**

   Divide the word into three groups of two letters each and write the letters of each group in the reverse order.

   $$\underline{\text{AN}} \; \underline{\text{SW}} \; \underline{\text{ER}} \to \underline{\text{NA}} \; \underline{\text{WS}} \; \underline{\text{RE}}$$
   $$\to \_\text{NBWTRF}$$

6. **(a)**

   Each letter in the word is replaced by the letter which occupies the same position from the other end of the alphabet, to obtain the code.

7. **(c)**

   All the letters of the word, except the last letter, are written in the reverse order and in the group of letters so obtained each letter is moved into steps forward to get the code.

   $$\text{AVOID} \to \text{IOVAD} \to \text{KQXCF.}$$

8. **(a)**

   $$\frac{\text{PO}}{1} \; \frac{\text{PU}}{2} \; \frac{\text{LA}}{3} \; \frac{\text{RI}}{4} \; \frac{\text{SE}}{5} \to \frac{\text{ES}}{5} \; \frac{\text{RI}}{4} \; \frac{\text{AL}}{3} \; \frac{\text{PU}}{2} \; \frac{\text{OP}}{1}$$

   Clearly, the sixth letter from the left in the code is L.

9. **(b)**

   Each letter of the word is five steps ahead the corresponding letter of the code.

10. **(d)**

    The code has been obtained by writing the first four and the last four letters of the word in the reverse order. Thus, we have.

    $$\text{SERPEVRE} \to \text{SERP/EVRE} \to \text{PRES/}$$
    $$\text{ERVE} \to \text{PRESERVE.}$$

11. **(a)**

    Letter : C O N E P T F R I D
    Code : u n m l q r y s g t
    The code for PREDICT is qsltgur.

12. **(c)**

    Letter: F I R E M O V
    Code: Q H O E Z M W
    The code for OVER is MWEO.

13. (b)

Each letter is coded by the numeral obtained by subtracting from 27 then numeral denoting the position of the letter in the English alphabet. W, O, M, A, N are 23rd, 15th, 13th, 1st and 14th letters. So their codes are (27 − 23), (27 − 15), (27 − 13), (27 − 1), (27 − 14) i.e. 4, 12, 14, 26, 13 respectively.

14. (c)

In the given code, Z = 1, Y = 2, X = 3, ……. C = 24, B = 25, Z = 26.

So, GO = 20 + 12 = 32 and SHE = 8 + 19 + 22 = 49.

Similarly, SOME = S + O + M + E = 8 + 12 + 14 + 22 = 56.

15. (c)

Taking

Z = 2, Y = 3, …., N = 14, ……, B = 26, A = 27

ZIP

= (Z + I + P) × 6 = (2 + 19 + 12) × 6 = 33 × 6 = 198

VIP

= (V + I + P) × 6 = (6 + 19 + 12) × 6 = 37 × 6 = 222

16. (b)

Let A = 1, B = 2, C = 3, ……, Z = 26.

Now, M = 13 = $\overline{4}$ (Remainder obtained after dividing by 9).

S = 19 = 1 (Remainder obtained after dividing by 9 twice)

T = 20 = 2 (Remainder obtained after dividing by 9 twice)

R = 18 = $\overline{9}$ (Remainder obtained after dividing by 9)

So, MASTER = $\overline{4}11259$, POWDER = 765459

17. (d)

Letter :	B	R	A	I	N	T	E
Code :	*	%	÷	#	×	$	+

The code for RENT is % + × .

18. (a)

Letter:	D	E	L	H	I	C	A	U	T
Code:	7	3	5	4	1	8	2	9	6

The code for CALICUT is 8251896.

19. (c)

Letter :	N	O	I	D	A
Code :	3	9	6	5	8

The code for INDIA is 63568.

20. (b)

Letter:	E	N	G	L	A	D	F	R	C
Code:	1	2	3	4	5	6	7	8	9

The code for GREECE is 381191.

21. (a)

Vowels A, E, I, O, U are coded as 1, 2, 3, 4, 5 respectively. Each of the consonants in the word is moved one step forward to give the corresponding letter of the code so, the code for ACID becomes ID3E.

22. (b)

Letter:	D	E	S	K	R	I
Code:	#		5	2	%	7

The code for RISK is % 752.

23. (d)

Letter:	E	A	T	C	H	I	R
Code:	3	1	8	2	4	5	6

The code for TEACHER is 8312436.

24. (c)

Letter:	D	E	A	F	I	L
Code:	3	5	8	7	4	6

The code for IDEAL is 43586.

25. (a)

CAR = (Number of letters in CAR) × 2
    = 3 × 2
    = 6

26. (d)

'Chillies' are green in colour and as given, 'chillies' are 'bananas'. So, 'bananas' are green in colour.

27. (c)

Birds fly in the 'sky' and as given, 'sky' is 'star'. So, birds fly in the 'star'.

28. **(a)**

The colour of milk is 'white'. But, as given 'green' means 'white'. So, the colour of milk is green.

29. **(b)**

A child will write with a 'pencil' and 'pencil' is called sharpener. So, a child will write with a 'sharpener'.

30. **(c)**

Fishes live in 'water' and as given, 'water' is called 'colour'. So, fishes live in 'colour'.

Alphabet Test

Alphabetical order means arrangement of words as they appear in the English dictionary. This is the order in which the beginning letters of these words appear in the English alphabet.

First, consider the first letter of each word, then second and so on and then arrange the words in the order in which the letters appear in English alphabet.

Example 1. Arrange the given words in alphabetical order.

Moment, Artist, Cricket, Patient, Worship, Neck.

The order of words as per English dictionary is as follows:

Artist, Cricket, Moment, Patient, Worship.

In some cases, two or more than two words begin with the same letter. Each word should be arranged in the order of second letters in the alphabet.

Example 2. Bucket, Parrot, Mirror, Memory, Crocon, Crowd, Cancel, Work, Nose.

The alphabetical order of the given words is as follows.

Bucket, Cancel, Crowd, Crown, Memory, Mirror, Nose, Parrot, Work.

If both the first and second letters of two or more words are the same, then arrange the words considering the third letters and so on. If first, second, and third letters of two or more words are the same, then arrange these words considering their fourth, letter and so on. In this way the words are arranged.

Alphabetical Order

Arranging words in alphabetical order implies 'to arrange them in the order as they appear in a dictionary' i.e., as per the order in which the beginning letters of these words appear in the English alphabet.

Direction (1 to 3): Arrange the given words in alphabetical order and choose the one that comes first.

Example 1:

	(a) Lesson	(b) Leopard
	(c) Language	(d) Lessen
Solution:	(c)	

Language, Leopard, Lessen, Lesson.

Example 2:

	(a) Rubber	(b) Rumple
	(c) Ruby	(d) Rumour
Solution:	(a)	

Rubber, Ruby, Rumour, Rumple.

Example 3:

	(a) Minority	(b) Miniature
	(c) Minister	(d) Minimalis
Solution:	(b)	

Miniature, Minimalis, Minister, Minority.

First consider the first letter of each word. Arrange the words in the order in which these letters appear in the English alphabet.

Direction (1 to 3): Arrange the given words in alphabetical order and choose the one that comes first.

Example 1:

    (a) Demand   (b) Diamond

    (c) Destroy   (d) Damage

Solution: (d)

    Damage, Demand, Destroy, Diamond.

Example 2:

    (a) School   (b) Science

    (c) Scissors   (d) Scorpion

Solution: (a)

    School, Science, Scissors, Scorpion.

Rule–Detection

Example 3:   Number of letters skipped in between the adjacent letters in the series are multiples of 3.

    (a) AELPZ   (b) LORUX

    (c) GKOTZ   (d) DHLPU

Solution: (a)

    [A] B C D [E] F G H I J K [L] M N O [P] Q R S T U V W X Y [Z]

          3   6   3   9

    3, 6, 9 are multiples of 3.

Example 4:   Number of letters skipped in between adjacent letters in the series is in the order of 1^2, 2^2, 3^2.

    (a) RTWZ   (b) CEJT

    (c) EGLP   (d) EGLO

Solution: (b)

    C D E F G H I J K L M N O P Q R S T

       1   4   9

Example 5:   Number of letters skipped in between the adjacent letters in the series is equal.

    (a) SUXADF   (b) RVZDHL

    (c) HKNGSH   (d) RVZDFG

Solution: (b)

    R S T U V W X Y Z A B C D E F G H I J K L

       3   3   3   3   3

Alphabetical Quibble

A letter series is given, be it the English alphabets from A to Z or a randomized sequence of letters. The candidate is then required to trace the letters satisfy certain given conditions as regards their position in the given sequence.

Example 6:   How many D's are there in the following series which are immediately followed by W but not immediately proceeded by k?

    K D C W K D W N K G D W W D H K V D W Z D W

    (a) Four   (b) Three

    (c) Two   (d) One

Solution: (b)

Clearly, D's satisfying the given conditions can be marked as under:

K D C W K D W N K G D W W D H K V D W Z D W.

We observe that such D' are three in number.

Example 7:   Which letter will be sixth to the left of the nineteenth letter from the right end of the alphabet?

(a) X   (b) Y

(c) M   (d) None of these

Solution: (d)

Counting right, i.e., from Z in the given alphabet series, the nineteenth letter is H.

Counting from H towards the left, the sixth letter is B.

Direction (1 to 6): Arrange the given words in alphabetical order and choose the one that comes first.

1.
   (a) Guarantee   (b) Group
   (c) Groan   (d) Grotesque

2.
   (a) Necessary   (b) Nature
   (c) Naval   (d) Nautical

3.
   (a) Foment   (b) Foetus
   (c) Foliage   (d) Forceps

4.
   (a) Deuce   (b) Dew
   (c) Devise   (d) Dexterity

5.
   (a) Quarter   (b) Quarrel
   (c) Quarry   (d) Qualify

6.
   (a) Probe   (b) Probate
   (c) Proceed   (d) Proclaim

Direction (7 to 13): Arrange the given words in the alphabetical order and choose the one that comes last.

7.
   (a) Fault   (b) Finger
   (c) Floor   (d) Forget

8.
   (a) Evolution   (b) Extra
   (c) Extreme   (d) Extraction

9.
   (a) Transport   (b) Transist
   (c) Transmit   (d) Translate

10.
   (a) Romance   (b) Roman
   (c) Rose   (d) Repeat

11.
   (a) Different   (b) Distance
   (c) Dialogue   (d) Diagonal

12.
   (a) Temperature   (b) Transition
   (c) Transmit   (d) Temple

13.
   (a) Warring   (b) Waving
   (c) Watching   (d) Waiting

Direction (14 to 20): In each of the following questions find out which of the letter series follows the given rule.

14. Number of letters skipped in between adjacent letters in the series is odd.
   (a) MPRUX   (b) FIMRX
   (c) EIMQV   (d) BDHLR

15. Number of letters skipped in between adjacent letters in the series is in the order of 2, 5, 7, 10.
   (a) QTZHS   (b) SYBEP
   (c) FNKOT   (d) CEGLT

16. Number of letters skipped in between adjacent letters in the series decreases by three.
   (a) HVDKP   (b) HUELP
   (c) HUELD   (d) DMSXA

17. Number of letters skipped in between adjacent letters in the series decreases by one each time.
   (a) BHNSV   (b) TZEIL
   (c) MSYBG   (d) IMTXB

18. Number of letters skipped in between adjacent letters in the series doubles every time.
   (a) BDGLU   (b) EGJOF
   (c) GJNSY   (d) ADIPY

19. Number of letters skipped in between adjacent letters of the series starting from behind increases by one.
   (a) ONLKJ   (b) OMKIG
   (c) OIGDC   (d) OMJFA

20. Number of letters skipped in between adjacent letters decrease in order.

   (a) SYDHK   (b) HNSWA
   (c) AGMRV   (d) NSXCH

Direction (21 to 30): Each of the following questions is based on the following alphabet – series:

A B C D E F G H I J K L M N O P Q R S T U V W X Y Z

21. Which letter is seventh to the right of the thirteenth letter from the left end?

   (a) S   (b) U
   (c) T   (d) None of these

22. Which letter in the alphabet is as far from G as T is from M?

   (a) P   (b) O
   (c) M   (d) N

23. Which letter is sixteenth to the right of the letter which is fourth to the left of I?

   (a) U   (b) V
   (c) T   (d) S

24. If the order of the English alphabet is reversed, then which letter would be exactly in the middle?

   (a) M   (b) N
   (c) L   (d) None of these

25. If only the first half of the given alphabet is reversed, how many letters will be there between K and R?

   (a) 14   (b) 16
   (c) 10   (d) 6

26. If the last ten letters of the alphabet are written in the reverse order, which of the following will be the sixth to the right of the thirteenth letter from the left end?

   (a) Y   (b) X
   (c) W   (d) V

27. A B C D E F G H I J K L M N O P Q R S T U V W X Y Z.

   Which letter is exactly midway between G and Q in the given alphabet?

   (a) K   (b) L
   (c) N   (d) M

28. If 1st and 26th, 2nd and 25th, 3rd and 24th and so on, letters of the English alphabet are paired, then which of the following pair is correct?

   (a) EV   (b) IP
   (c) GR   (d) CW

29. If in the English alphabet every fourth letter is replaced by the symbol (∗), which of the following would be seventh to the left of the fourteenth element from the left?

   (a) ∗   (b) T
   (c) H   (d) G

30. In the following alphabets, which letter is eighth to the right of the fourteenth letter from the right end?

   Z A B C D E F G H I J K L M N O P Q R S T U V W X Y

   (a) H   (b) R
   (c) S   (d) T

Answer Key

1. (c)	2. (b)	3. (b)	4. (a)	5. (d)	6. (b)	7. (d)	8. (c)	9. (b)	10. (c)
11. (b)	12. (d)	13. (b)	14. (d)	15. (a)	16. (b)	17. (b)	18. (a)	19. (d)	20. (a)
21. (c)	22. (d)	23. (a)	24. (d)	25. (a)	26. (b)	27. (b)	28. (a)	29. (d)	30. (d)

Hints and Solutions

1. **(c)**
   Groan, Grotesque, Group, Guarantee.

2. **(b)**
   Nature, Nautical, Naval, Necessary.

3. **(b)**
   Foetus, Foliage, Foment, Forceps.

4. **(a)**
   Deuce, Devise, Dew, Dexterity.

5. **(d)**
   Qualify, Quarrel, Quarry, Quarter.

6. **(b)**
   Probate, Probe, Proceed, Proclaim.

7. **(d)**
   Fault, Finger, Floor, Forget.

8. **(c)**
   Evolution, Extra, Extraction, Extreme.

9. **(b)**
   Translate, Transmit, Transport, Transist.

10. **(c)**
    Repeat, Roman, Romance, Rose.

11. **(b)**
    Diagonal, Dialogue, Different, Distance.

12. **(d)**
    Transition, Transmit, Temperature, Temple.

13. **(b)**
    Waiting, Warring, Watching, Waving.

14. **(d)**
    B C D E F G H I J K L M N O P Q R
       1   3   3   5

    1, 3, 5 are all odd numbers.

15. **(a)**
    Q R S T U V W X Y Z A B C D E F G
      2   5   7

    H I J K L M N O P Q R S
           10

16. **(b)**
    H I J K L M N O P Q R S T U V W X Y Z
         12   9

A B C D [E] F G H I J K [L] M N O [P]
         6   3

17. **(b)**
    [T] U V W X Y [Z] A B C D [E] F G H [I] J K [L]
      5   4   3   2

18. **(a)**
    [B] [C] D E F [G] H I J K [L] M N O P Q R S T [U]
     1   2   4   8

19. **(d)**
    [O] N [M] L K [J] I H G [F] E D C B [A]
     1   2   3   4

20. **(a)**
    [S] T U V W X [Y] Z A B C [D] E F G [H] I J [K]
     5   4   3   2

21. **(c)**
    Counting from the left, i.e. from A in the given alphabet series, the thirteenth letter is M. counting from M towards the right, the seventh letter is T.

22. **(d)**
    T is seventh letter to the right of M. Similarly, the seventh letter to the right of G is N.

23. **(a)**
    The fourth letter to the left of I is E. the sixteenth letter to the right of E is U.

24. **(d)**
    The new letter series obtained on reversing the order of the English alphabet is

    Z Y X W V U T S R Q P O N M L K J I H G F E D C B A.

    Since the series has an even number of letters there is no such letter which lies exactly in the middle.

25. **(a)**
    Reversing only the first 13 letters, we obtain the following letter series:

    M L K J I H G F E D C B A N O P Q R S T U V W X Y Z.

    Clearly, there are 14 letters between K and R in the above series.

26. **(b)**

The new alphabet series is:

A B C D E F G H I J K L M N O P Z Y X W
V U T S R Q

The thirteenth letter from the left is M. The sixth letter to the right of M is X.

27. **(b)**

There are nine letters between G and Q – H, I, J, K, L, M, N, O, P. Clearly, the middle letter is L.

28. **(a)**

The pairing up of letters may be done as shown.

AZ, BY, CX, DW, EV, FU, GT, HS, IR, JQ, KP, LO, MN.

29. **(d)**

The new series becomes

A B C * E F G * I J K * M N O * Q R S * U
V W * YZ.

30. **(d)**

The fourteenth letter from the right is L. the eighth letter to the right of L is T.

Number and Ranking Test

The problems based on Number Ranking consist of a set, group or series of numerals. The candidate has to trace out the numerals following some certain given conditions or lying at particular specified position according to a certain given pattern. For this, he/she has to analyse the given series of numerals or number sequence and study the pattern to answer the appropriate option.

In the number sequence a number which comes after a given number is said to follow it while the number which comes before the given number precedes it.

The problems such as a number in between two odd numbers or two even numbers or a number in between two of its factors are based on the number test.

Number Test

In this type of questions, a series of numbers is given. The students to study the series and answer the given questions according to the given conditions.

Ranking Test

In this test the rank of a person from the top and from the bottom is mentioned and the candidate has to find out total number of persons.

In some problems, the test is in the form of puzzle of interchanging positions by two persons. In the ranking problems, the student has to find out the total number of persons, position of particular person from left end or right end.

Example 1: In the given series, how many 7's are there which is preceded by 5 and followed by 3?

4 2 7 6 5 7 3 8 9 5 7 3 4 6 7 5 3 4 6

(a) 1   (b) 2   (c) 3   (d) 4

Solution: (b)

4 2 7 6 5 7 3 8 9 5 7 3 4 6 7 5 3 4 6

Example 2: How many 8's are there which is exactly divisible by its immediate preceding as well as successing numbers?

2 8 3 8 2 4 8 6 4 8 6 8 2 8 2 4 8 3 8 2 8 6

(a) 1   (b) 2   (c) 3   (d) 4

Solution: (b)

2 8 3 8 2 4 8 6 4 8 6 8 2 8 2 4 8 3 8 2 8 6

Example 3: How many 5's are there which is exactly preceding by 1 and followed by 2?

6 4 2 3 1 5 2 6 8 9 5 4 3 1 5 2 7 8 9 5 4 3 6

(a) 1   (b) 2   (c) 3   (d) 4

Solution: (b)

6 4 2 3 1 5 2 6 8 9 5 4 3 1 5 2 7 8 9 5 4 3 6

Example 4: Mohit is 14th from the right end in a row of 40 students. What is his position from the left end?

(a) 1 (b) 2 (c) 3 (d) 4

Solution: (c)

Number of students towards the left of Mohit = 40 − 14 = 26.

So, his position is (26 + 1)th = 27th from left.

Example 5: Mohan ranks 8th from the top and 32th from the bottom in a class. How many students are there in class?

(a) 1 (b) 2 (c) 3 (d) 4

Solution: (b)

No. of students in the class = 8 + 32 − 1 = 39

1. In the series given below, how many 8's are there each of which is exactly divisible by its immediate preceding as well as succeeding numbers?

   2 8 4 3 8 5 4 8 2 6 7 8 4 6 2 8 4 1 7 ?

   (a) 1   (b) 2
   (c) 3   (d) 4

2. How many 5's are there in the following number sequence which are immediately preceded by 7 and immediately followed by 8?

   7 5 5 8 4 5 7 8 4 5 9 8 7 5 8 7 8 4 3 2 5 8 7 6?

   (a) 1   (b) 2
   (c) 3   (d) None of these

3. In the given series 7 4 5 7 6 8 4 2 1 3 5 1 7 6 8 9 2 how many pairs of alternate numbers have a difference of 2?

   (a) 1   (b) 2
   (c) 3   (d) 4

4. How many 4's are there preceded by 7 but not followed by 5?

   5 9 3 1 7 4 5 8 4 6 7 4 3 1 4 7 4 2 8 7 4 1 ?

   (a) 1   (b) 2
   (c) 3   (d) 4

5. How many 5's are there which are in between two even numbers.

   4 3 5 6 4 5 2 3 4 5 8 5 4 6 7 5 2 6 9 8 5 1 2 4 5

   (a) 1   (b) 2
   (c) 3   (d) 4

6. How many 3's are there preceded by 2 but not followed by 7.

   1 2 3 7 4 3 2 5 6 7 2 8 9 6 4 3 2 5 6 8 4 6 8 2 3 4

   (a) 1   (b) 2
   (c) 3   (d) 4

7. In how many terms, the difference between two consecutive terms is 3?

   8 5 2 4 1 6 2 7 6 4 1 3 5 2 5 7 4 1 8 9 6 2 5 6 9 4 1

8. In how many times, between two odd numbers, there is an even number?

   4 6 3 4 7 2 5 4 1 2 3 4 5 6 7 8 9 6 4 7 5 2 ?

   (a) 5   (b) 6
   (c) 7   (d) 8

9. In how many times, the sum of two consecutive terms is 7?

   4 2 5 1 6 4 3 8 1 9 4 5 2 3 4 1 6 7 4 5 3 4 5 6 2

   (a) 4   (b) 5
   (c) 6   (d) 7

10. How many times the difference between two consecutive terms is 5?

    1 3 4 6 9 8 4 2 7 6 4 9 6 3 8 2 6 4 1 6 7 4

    (a) 3   (b) 4
    (c) 5   (d) 6

11. Ranjan ranks 18th in a class of 49 students. What is his rank from last?

    (a) 28   (b) 29
    (c) 31   (d) 32

12. If Aman finds that he is 12th from the right in a line of boys and 4th from the left. How many boys should be added to the line such that there are 35 students in the line?

    (a) 18   (b) 19
    (c) 20   (d) 21

13. In a queue, Ravi is 13th from the back Amar is 12th from the front. Hari is standing between the two. What should be the minimum number of boys standing in queue?

    (a) 14   (b) 15
    (c) 16   (d) 17

14. In a row of boys Raja is 10th from the left and Pramod, who is 9th from the right interchange their positions, Raja becomes 15th from the left. How many boys are there in the row?

    (a) 23   (b) 24
    (c) 25   (d) 26

15. Shankar ranked 7th from the top and 34th from the bottom in a class. How many students are there in a class?
    (a) 38
    (b) 39
    (c) 40
    (d) 41

16. Saket is 7 ranks ahead of Manoj in a class of 50. If Manoj's rank is 17th from the last, what is Saket's rank from the start?
    (a) 25
    (b) 26
    (c) 27
    (d) 28

17. If in a single line, Mohan is 23rd from both the ends. How many boys are there in the class?
    (a) 44
    (b) 45
    (c) 46
    (d) 47

18. Naresh ranks 5th in a class, Vikas is 8th from the last. If Raju is 6th after Naresh and Just in the middle of Naresh and Vikas. How many students are there in the class?
    (a) 23
    (b) 24
    (c) 25
    (d) 26

19. Ashok is 8th from the left and Sanjay is 14th from the right end in a row of boys. If there are 12 boys between Ashok and Sanjay, how many boys are there in the row?
    (a) 32
    (b) 33
    (c) 34
    (d) 35

20. If the numbers from 1 to 100, which are exactly divisible by 5 are arranged in descending order, which would come at the 11th position from the bottom?
    (a) 50
    (b) 55
    (c) 60
    (d) 65

21. How many numbers from 11 to 100 which are exactly divisible by 7 but not by 3?
    (a) 9
    (b) 8
    (c) 7
    (d) 10

22. How many numbers from 1 to 100, which are exactly divisible by 15 but not by 5?
    (a) 5
    (b) 6
    (c) 7
    (d) None of these

23. If the following series is written in reverse order, which number will be 4th to the right of the 7th number from the left?

    7, 3, 9, 7, 1, 3, 8, 4, 6, 2, 1, 8, 5, 11, 13
    (a) 1
    (b) 3
    (c) 7
    (d) 8

24. In the given sequence, how many such even numbers are there which are exactly divisible by its immediate preceding number, but not exactly divisible by its immediate following number?

    3 8 4 1 5 7 2 8 3 4 8 9 3 9 4 2 1 5 8 2
    (a) 1
    (b) 2
    (c) 3
    (d) 4

Answer Key

1. (c)	2. (a)	3. (c)	4. (c)	5. (c)	6. (a)	7. (d)	8. (c)	9. (d)	10. (b)
11. (d)	12. (c)	13. (a)	14. (a)	15. (c)	16. (c)	17. (b)	18. (b)	19. (c)	20. (b)
21. (b)	22. (d)	23. (a)	24. (b)						

Hints *and* Solutions

1. **(c)** The given series is

   2 8 4 3 8 5 4 8 2 6 7 8 4 6 2 8 4 1 7

3. **(c)** The given series is

   7 4 5 7 6 8 4 2 1 3 5 1 7 6 8 9 2

4. **(c)** The given series is

   5 9 3 1 7 4 5 8 4 6 7 4 3 1 4 7 4 2 8 7 4 1

5. **(c)** The given series is

   4 3 5 6 4 5 2 3 4 5 8 5 4 6 7 5 2 6 9 8 5 1 2 4 5

6. **(a)** The given series is

   1 2 3 7 4 3 2 5 6 7 2 8 9 6 4 3 2 5 6 8 4 6 8 2 3 4

11. **(d)** Here, 49 – 18 = 31

    So, Ranjan's rank = 31 + 1 = 32nd form the last.

12. **(c)** No. of boys in the line = 12 + 4 – 1 = 15.

    No. of boys to be added = 35 – 15 = 20

13. **(a)**

    1 2 3 4 5 6 7 8 9 10 11 12 13

    ↑   ↑

    Ravi   Amar

    Minimum no. of boys = 13 + 1 = 14

14. **(a)** Raja's new position is 15th from the left and

this is the same as 9th position from the right for Pramod.

No. of boys = 15 + 9 – 1 = 23

15. **(c)** Total number of students = 6 + 1 + 33 = 40

16. **(c)** Manoj's rank is 17th from the last.

    Saket's rank = 17 + 7 = 24th from the last.

    No. of students ahead of Saket = 50 – 24 = 26

    Saket's rank from start = 26 + 1 = 27th

17. **(b)** Required no. of boys = 22 + 1 + 22 = 45

18. **(b)** Total no. of students = 5 + 6 + 6 + 8 – 1 = 24

19. **(c)** Number of boys = 8 + 14 + 12 = 34

20. **(b)** 95, 90, 85, 80, 75, 70, 65, 60, **55**, 50, 45, 40, 35, 30, 25, 20, 15, 10, 5

21. **(a)** The numbers are 14, 28, 35, 49, 56, 70, 77, 91, 98

22. **(d)** Not possible

23. **(a)**

    13, 11, 5, 8, 1, 2, 6, 4, 8, 3, 1, 7, 9, 3, 7

    ↑   ↑

24. **(b)**

    3 8 4 1 5 7 2 8 3 4 8 9 3 9 4 2 1 5 8 2

The questions on Directions Sense are based on various directions called direction puzzles. The figure given below shows four main directions namely North, South, East and West. There are four cardinal directions namely North – East (NE), North – West (NW), South – East (SE) and South – West (SW).

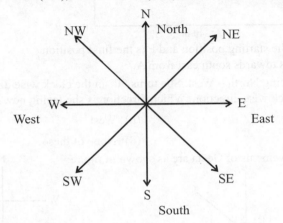

In this type of questions, a successive follow up of directions is formulated. The candidate is required to decide the final direction or distance between starting and end points. Direction Sense Test is basically hold to check the candidate's ability to trace and follow the direction correctly.

The candidate is required to trace the diagram and find out the distance between initial point and final point. He/she has to analyse directions carefully and answer the questions. The diagram is very essential in direction sense problems.

Example 1: Mohan faces towards north. Turning to his right, he walks 25m. He then turns to his left and walks 30m. Next he moves 25m to his right. He then turns to his right again and walks 55m. At last, he turns to his right and moves 40m. In which direction is he now from his starting point?

    (a)   SE   (b)   NE

    (c)   South   (d)   East

Solution: (a) The movements of the Mohan are as shown below:

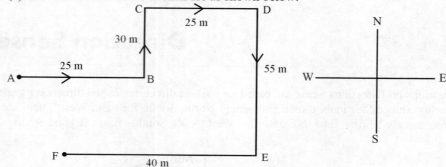

Here, A is the starting position and F is the final position.

Clearly, F is towards south east from A.

Example 2: Geeta is facing North – West. She turns 90° in the clock wise direction and then 135° in the anti clock wise direction. Which direction is she facing now?

(a) East
(b) West
(c) North
(d) None of these

Solution: (b) The movements of Geeta are as shown in figure:

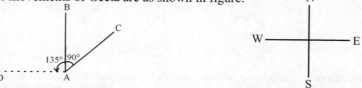

Starting point is A. Initially she is facing AB. Finally the position is AD, which is west from starting position.

Example 3: Sohan walks 30 m towards south then turning to his right he walks 30 m, then turning to his left he walks 20 m, Again he turns to his left and walks 30 m. How far is he from his starting position?

(a) 30 m
(b) 40 m
(c) 50 m
(d) 60 m

Solution: (c) The movements of Sohan are as shown below:

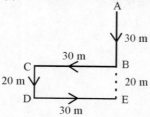

Starting point A, Final Point E.

AE = AB + BE = AB + CD
   = 30 + 20 = 50m

1. One morning after sunrise, Mohan was standing facing a pole. The shadow of the pole fall exactly to his right. Which direction was he facing?
   (a) North   (b) South
   (c) East   (d) West

2. If south – east is called east, north – west is called west, south – west is called south and so on what will north be called?
   (a) South   (b) North East
   (c) East   (d) North West

3. A, B, C and D are playing a game of carom. A & C and B & D are partners. D is to the right of C, who is facing west, then in which direction B is facing?
   (a) East   (b) West
   (c) North   (d) South

4. Rajesh is 40m south – west of Rohit. Rakesh is 40m south-east of Rohit. Then Rakesh is in which direction of Rajesh?
   (a) East   (b) West
   (c) South   (d) North

5. Pravin wants to go to the college. He starts from his home which is in the east and comes to a crossing. The road to the left ends in a theatre, straight ahead in the hospital. In which direction is the college?
   (a) North   (b) South
   (c) East   (d) West

6. Naresh walks 30 m towards south. Then turning to his right, he walks 30 m then turning to his left, he walks 20 m. Again he turns to his left and walked 30 m. How far is he from his initial position?
   (a) 30 m   (b) 40 m
   (c) 50 m   (d) 60 m

7. Manoj walks 10 m in front end 10m to the right then every time turning to his left. He walks 5 m, 15 m and 15 m respectively. How far is he now from his starting point?
   (a) 5 m   (b) 10 m
   (c) 15 m   (d) 20 m

8. Nilesh went 15 km to the west from my house then turned left and walked 20 km. Then turned east and walked 25 km and finally turning left covered 20 km. How far was he from his house?
   (a) 5 km   (b) 10 km
   (c) 60 km   (d) 40 km

9. Geeta walks Northwards. After a while, she turns to her right and a little further to her left. Finally after walking a distance of 0.5km, she turns to her left again. In which direction is she moving now?
   (a) East   (b) West
   (c) North   (d) South

10. Kishan walked 40 m towards East, took a right turn and walked 50 m. Then he took a left turn and walked 40 m. in which direction is he now from the starting point?
    (a) East   (b) South
    (c) North-east   (d) South-east

11. Mahesh goes 30 m North then turns right and walks 40 m then again turns right and walks 20 m then again turns right and walks 40m. How many metres is he from his starting position.
    (a) 10 m   (b) 15 m
    (c) 20 m   (d) 30 m

12. A, B, C, D, E, F, G, H are sitting around a round table in the same order at equal distance for group discussion. Their positions are clockwise. If G sits in the north then what will be the position of D?
    (a) South east   (b) South west
    (c) South   (d) East

13. If P is to south of Q and R is to the east of Q. In which direction is P with respect to R?
    (a) North-East   (b) North-West
    (c) South-East   (d) South-West

14. Ramesh is performing yoga with his head down and legs up. His face is towards the west. In which direction will his left hand be?

(a) East   (b) West

(c) South   (d) North

15. A clock is so placed that at 12 noon its minute hand points towards north-east. In what direction does its hour hand point at 1.30 P.M. ?

(a) East   (b) West

(c) North   (d) South

16. Rohan is facing North. He turns 135° in the anticlockwise direction and then 180° in the clockwise direction. Which direction is he facing now?

(a) NE   (b) NW

(c) SW   (d) SE

17. Ritesh went to meet his cousin to another village situated 5 km away in north-east direction of Ritesh's village. From there he came to meet his friend living in a village situated 4 km in the south of his cousin's village. How far away and in which direction is he now?

(a) 3 km, East   (b) 4 km, East

(c) 3 km, North   (d) 4 km, West

18. Karim goes 30 m North then turns right and walks 40 m then again turns right and walks 20 m, then again turns right and walks 40m. How far is he from his original position?

(a) 10 m   (b) 20 m

(c) 25 m   (d) 40 m

19. Ankur walked 30 m towards east, took a right turn and walked 40 m. then took a left turn and walked 30 m. In which direction is he now from the starting point?

(a) South   (b) South-east

(c) East   (d) North-east

20. Rohit went 15 km to the west from my house then turned left and walked 20 km. he then turned east and walked 25 km and finally turning left covered 20 km. How far was he from his house?

(a) 10 km   (b) 15 km

(c) 20 km   (d) 40 km

Answer Key

1. (b)	2. (d)	3. (c)	4. (a)	5. (a)	6. (c)	7. (a)	8. (b)	9. (b)	10 (d)
11. (a)	12. (b)	13. (d)	14. (d)	15. (a)	16. (c)	17. (a)	18. (a)	19. (b)	20. (a)

Hints and Solutions

1. (b)

Sun rises in the east in the morning. So, in morning, the shadow falls towards the west. Now, Mohan's shadow falls to his right. So, he is standing, facing south.

2. (d)

In diagram (A) the directions are shown as they actually are. Diagram (B) is as per the given data. So, comparing the direction of north in (A) with that in (B), north will be called north west.

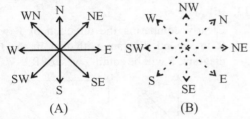

(A)   (B)

3. (c)

As per the given data, C faces north. A faces towards west. D is to the right of C. So, D is facing towards south. Thus, B who is the partner of D will face towards north.

4. (a)

It is clear from the adjoining diagram that Rakesh lies to the east of Rajesh.

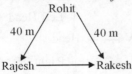

5. (a)

Starting from his house in the East, Pravin moves west wards. Then, the theatre, which is the left, will be in the south. The hospital, which is straight ahead, will be to the west. So, the college will be to the north.

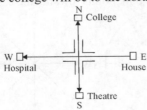

6. (c)

The movments of the Naresh are as shown in figure

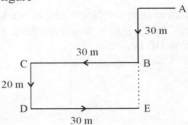

∴ Naresh's distance from initial position A

= AE = (AB + BE) = (AB + CD)

= (30 + 20) m

= 50m

7. (a)

The movements of Manoj are as shown in figure (O to P, P to Q, Q to R, R to S and S to T).

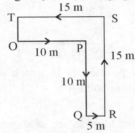

Since TS = OP + QR, so T lies with O.

∴ Required distance

OT = (RS – PQ)

= (15 – 10) m

= 5 m

8. (b)

The movements of Nilesh are as shown in figure

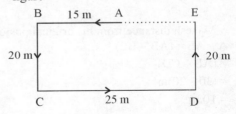

∴ Nilesh distance from his house at A.

AE = (BE − BA)
   = (CD − BA)
   = (25 − 15) m
   = 10 m

9. (b)

The movements of Geeta are as shown in figure. Clearly she is finally walking in the direction DE i.e, west.

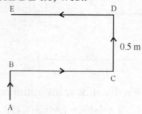

10. (d)

The movements of Kishan are as shown in figure (A to B, B to C, C to D).

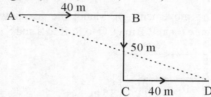

Clearly his final position is D which is to south-east of starting point A.

11. (a)

The movements of Mahesh are as shown in figure (A to B, B to C, C to D, D to E).

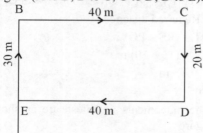

∴ Mahesh distance from his original position
A = AE = (AB − BE)
= (AB − CD)
= (30 − 20)m
= 10 m

12. (b)

Clearly, the seating arrangement is as shown in the adjoining figure.

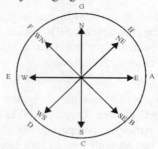

So, D is at the south west position.

13. (d)

Clearly comparing the direction of P w.r.t. R in second diagram with that in the first diagram, P will be south – west of R.

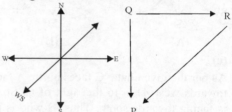

14. (d)

The posture of the Ramesh is as shown. Clearly, the left hand points towards north.

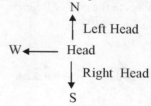

15. (a)

Clearly, the positions of the minute and hour hands at 12 noon and 1.30 p.m. are as shown in the diagram. So, as shown, the hour hand at 1.30 p.m. points towards the east.

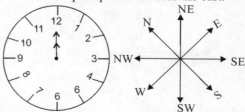

16. (c)

Rohan initially faces in the direction OA. On moving 135° anti clockwise, he faces in the direction OB. On further moving 180° clockwise, he faces on the direction OC, which is south west, as shown in figure

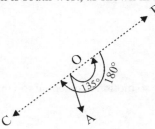

17. (a)

Ritesh moves from his village at O to his uncle's village at A and thereon to his father in law village at B.

Clearly, ΔOBA is right-angled at B.

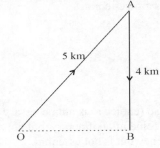

So, $OA^2 = OB^2 + AB^2$

$\Rightarrow OB^2 = OA^2 - AB^2$

$\Rightarrow OB = \sqrt{(25-16)}$ km $= \sqrt{(9)}$ km = 3km.

Thus B is 3 km to the east of his initial position O.

18. (a)

The movements of Karim are as shown in figure

(A to B, B to C, C to D, D to E).

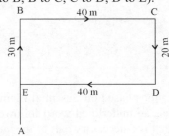

∴ Karim's distance from his original position

A = AE = (AB – BE)

= (AB – CD)

= (30 – 20) m

= 10 m

19. (b)

The movements of Ankur are as shown in figure (P to Q, Q to R and R to S). Clearly, his final position is S which is to the south east of the starting point P.

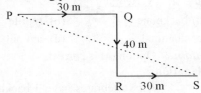

20. (a)

The movements of Rohit are as shown in figure

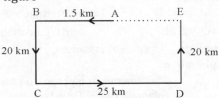

∴ Rohit's distance from his house at A

AE = (BE – BA)

= (CD – BA)

= (25 – 15) km

= 10 km

9   Essential Element

In the questions based on Essential Element the student will find an essential part of something. Each question has an underlined word followed by four answer choices. The student is required to choose the word that is a necessary part of the underlined word. A good approach could be to say the following sentence: "A _____ could not exist without _____." Put the underlined word in the first blank. Try each of the answer choices in the second blank to see which choice is most logical.

Direction (1 to 3): Find the word that names a necessary part of the underlined word.

Example 1:   Vibration

     (a) motion   (b) electricity

     (c) science   (d) sound

   Solution: Option (a) is correct.

Explanation:

         Anything cannot vibrate without creating motion, so motion is essential to vibration.

Example 2:   Vertebrate

     (a) backbone   (b) reptile

     (c) mammal   (d) animal

   Solution: Option (a) is correct.

Explanation:

         All vertebrates have a backbone. Reptiles (choice b) are vertebrates, but so are many other animals. Mammals (choice c) are vertebrates, but so are birds and reptiles. All vertebrates (choice d) are animals, but not all animals are vertebrates.

Example 3:   Itinerary

     (a) map   (b) route

     (c) travel   (d) guidebook

   Solution: Option (b) is correct.

Explanation:

         An itinerary is a proposed route of a journey. A map (choice a) is not necessary to have a planned route. Travel (choice c) is usually the outcome of an itinerary, but not always. A guidebook (choice d) may be used to plan the journey but is not essential.

Direction (1 to 30):

Find the word that names a necessary part of the underlined word.

1. Knowledge
   - (a) School
   - (b) Teacher
   - (c) Textbook
   - (d) Learning

2. Culture
   - (a) Civility
   - (b) Education
   - (c) Agriculture
   - (d) Customs

3. Antique
   - (a) Rarity
   - (b) Artefact
   - (c) Aged
   - (d) Prehistoric

4. Dimension
   - (a) Compass
   - (b) Ruler
   - (c) Inch
   - (d) Measure

5. Purchase
   - (a) Trade
   - (b) Money
   - (c) Bank
   - (d) Acquisition

6. Infirmary
   - (a) Surgery
   - (b) Disease
   - (c) Patient
   - (d) Receptionist

7. Sustenance
   - (a) Nourishment
   - (b) Water
   - (c) Grains
   - (d) Menu

8. Provisions
   - (a) Groceries
   - (b) Supplies
   - (c) Gear
   - (d) Caterers

9. School
   - (a) Student
   - (b) Report card
   - (c) Test
   - (d) Learning

10. Language
    - (a) Tongue
    - (b) Slang
    - (c) Writing
    - (d) Words

11. Book
    - (a) Fiction
    - (b) Pages
    - (c) Pictures
    - (d) Learning

12. Desert
    - (a) Cactus
    - (b) Arid
    - (c) Oasis
    - (d) Flat

13. Lightning
    - (a) Electricity
    - (b) Thunder
    - (c) Brightness
    - (d) Rain

14. Swimming
    - (a) Pool
    - (b) Bathing suit
    - (c) Water
    - (d) Life jacket

15. Shoe
    - (a) Sole
    - (b) Leather
    - (c) Laces
    - (d) Walking

16. Ovation
    - (a) Outburst
    - (b) Bravo
    - (c) Applause
    - (d) Encore

17. Bonus
    - (a) Reward
    - (b) Raise
    - (c) Cash
    - (d) Employer

18. Cage
    - (a) Enclosure
    - (b) Prisoner
    - (c) Animal
    - (d) Zoo

19. Wedding
    - (a) Love
    - (b) Church
    - (c) Ring
    - (d) Marriage

20. Faculty
    - (a) Buildings
    - (b) Textbooks
    - (c) Teachers
    - (d) Meetings

21. Recipe
    - (a) Desserts
    - (b) Directions
    - (c) Cookbook
    - (d) Utensils

22. Autograph
    - (a) Athlete
    - (b) Actor
    - (c) Signature
    - (d) Pen

23. Champion
    - (a) Running
    - (b) Swimming
    - (c) Winning
    - (d) Speaking

24. Saddle
    - (a) Horse
    - (b) Seat
    - (c) Stirrups
    - (d) Horn

25. Dome
    - (a) Rounded
    - (b) Geodesic
    - (c) Governmental
    - (d) Coppery

26. Glacier
    - (a) Mountain
    - (b) Winter
    - (c) Prehistory
    - (d) Ice

27. Directory
    - (a) Telephone
    - (b) Listing
    - (c) Computer
    - (d) Names

28. Contract
    - (a) Agreement
    - (b) Document
    - (c) Written
    - (d) Attorney

29. Hurricane
    - (a) Beach
    - (b) Cyclone
    - (c) Damage
    - (d) Wind

30. Town
    - (a) Residents
    - (b) Skyscrapers
    - (c) Parks
    - (d) Libraries

Answer Key

1. (d)	2. (d)	3. (c)	4. (d)	5. (d)	6. (c)	7. (a)	8. (b)
9. (a)	10. (d)	11. (b)	12. (b)	13. (a)	14. (c)	15. (a)	16. (c)
17. (a)	18. (a)	19. (d)	20. (c)	21. (b)	22. (c)	23. (c)	24. (b)
25. (a)	26. (d)	27. (b)	28. (a)	29. (d)	30. (a)		

1. **(d)**
   Knowledge is gained through experience or study, so learning is the essential element. A school (choice a) is not necessary for learning or knowledge to take place, nor is a teacher or a textbook (choices b and c).

2. **(d)**
   A culture is the behaviour pattern of a particular population, so customs are the essential element. A culture may or may not be civil or educated (choices a and b). A culture may be an agricultural society (choice c), but this is not the essential element.

3. **(c)**
   An antique is something that belongs to, or was made in, an earlier period. It may or may not be a rarity (choice a), and it cannot be an artifact, an object produced or shaped by human craft (choice b). An antique is old but does not have to be prehistoric (choice d).

4. **(d)**
   A dimension is a measure of spatial content. A compass (choice a) and ruler (choice b) may help determine the dimension, but other instruments may also be used, so these are not the essential element here. An inch (choice c) is only one way to determine a dimension.

5. **(d)**
   A purchase is an acquisition of something. A purchase may be made by trade (choice a) or with money (choice b), so those are not essential elements. A bank (choice c) may or may not be involved in a purchase.

6. **(c)**
   An infirmary is a place that takes care of the infirm, sick, or injured. Without patients, there is no infirmary. Surgery (choice a) may not be required for patients. A disease (choice b) is not necessary because the infirmary may only see patients with injuries. A receptionist (choice d) would be helpful but not essential.

7. **(a)**
   Sustenance is something, especially food, that sustains life or health, so nourishment is the essential element. Water and grains (choices b and c) are components of nourishment, but other things can be taken in as well. A menu (choice d) may present a list of foods, but it is not essential to sustenance.

8. **(b)**
   Provisions imply the general supplies needed, so choice b is the essential element. The other choices are by products, but they are not essential.

9. **(a)**
   Without students, a school cannot exist; therefore, students are the essential part of schools. The other choices may be related, but they are not essential.

10. **(d)**
    Words are a necessary part of language. Slang is not necessary to language (choice b). Not all languages are written (choice c). Words do not have to be spoken in order to be part of a language (choice a).

11. **(b)**
    The necessary part of a book is its pages; there is no book without pages. Not all books are fiction (choice a), and not all books have pictures (choice c). Learning (choice d) may or may not take place with a book.

12. **(b)**
    A desert is an arid tract of land. Not all deserts are flat (choice d). Not all deserts have cacti or oases (choices a and c).

13. **(a)**
    Lightning is produced from a discharge of electricity, so electricity is essential. Thunder and rain are not essential to the production of lightning (choices b and d). Brightness may be a by-product of lightning, but it is not essential (choice c).

14. **(c)**

Water is essential for swimming; without water, there is no swimming. The other choices are things that may or may not be present.

15. **(a)**

All shoes have a sole of some sort. Not all shoes are made of leather (choice b); nor do they all have laces (choice c).Walking (choice d) is not essential to a shoe.

16. **(c)**

An ovation is prolonged, enthusiastic applause, so applause is necessary to an ovation. An outburst (choice a) may take place during an ovation; "bravo" (choice b) may or may not be uttered; and an encore (choice d) would take place after an ovation.

17. **(a)**

A bonus is something given or paid beyond what is usual or expected, so reward is the essential element. A bonus may not involve a raise in pay or cash (choices b and c), and it may be received from someone other than an employer (choice d).

18. **(a)**

A cage is meant to keep something surrounded, so enclosure is the essential element. A prisoner (choice b) or an animal (choice c) are two things that may be kept in cages, among many other things. A zoo (choice d) is only one place that has cages.

19. **(d)**

A wedding results in a marriage, so choice d is the essential element. Love (choice a) usually precedes a wedding, but it is not essential. A wedding may take place anywhere, so a church (choice b) is not required. A ring (choice c) is often used in a wedding, but it is not necessary.

20. **(c)**

A faculty consists of a group of teachers and cannot exist without them. The faculty may work in buildings (choice a), but the buildings aren't essential. They may use textbooks (choice b) and attend meetings (choice d), but these aren't essential.

21. **(b)**

A recipe is a list of directions to make something. Recipes may be used to prepare desserts (choice a), among other things. One does not need a cookbook (choice c) to have a recipe, and utensils (choice d) may or may not be used to make a recipe.

22. **(c)**

Without a signature, there is no autograph. Athletes and actors (choices a and b) may sign autographs, but they are not essential. An autograph can be signed with something other than a pen (choice d).

23. **(c)**

Without a first-place win, there is no champion, so winning is essential. There may be champions in running, swimming, or speaking, but there are also champions in many other areas.

24. **(b)**

A saddle is something one uses to sit on an animal, so it must have a seat (choice b). A saddle is often used on a horse (choice a), but it may be used on other animals. Stirrups (choice c) are often found on a saddle but can not be used. A horn (choice d) is found on Western saddles, but not on English saddles, so it is not the essential element here.

25. **(a)**

A dome is a large rounded roof or ceiling, so being rounded is essential to a dome. A geodesic dome (choice b) is only one type of dome. Some, but not all domes, have copper roofs (choice d). Domes are often found on government buildings (choice c), but domes exist at many other places.

26. **(d)**

A glacier is a large mass of ice and cannot exist without it. A glacier can move down a mountain, but it can also move across a valley or a plain, which rules out choice a. Glaciers exist in all seasons, which rules out choice b. There are many glaciers in the world today, which rules out choice c.

27. **(b)**

A directory is a listing of names or things, so (choice b) is the essential element. A telephone (choice a) often has a directory associated with it, but it is not essential. A computer (choice c) uses a directory format to list files, but it is not required. Names (choice d) are often listed in a directory, but many other things are listed in directories, so this is not the essential element.

28. **(a)**

An agreement is necessary to have a contract. A contract may appear on a document (choice b), but it is not required. A contract may be oral as well as written, so choice c is not essential. A contract can be made without an attorney (choice d).

29. **(d)**

A hurricane cannot exist without wind. A beach is not essential to a hurricane (choice a). A hurricane is a type of cyclone, which rules out (choice b). Not all hurricanes cause damage (choice c).

30. **(a)**

Residents must be present in order to have a town. A town may be too small to have skyscrapers (choice b). A town may or may not have parks (choice c) and libraries (choice d), so they are not the essential elements.

Mirror Image

The image of an object, as seen in a mirror, is called its mirror reflection or mirror image.

In such an image, the right side of the object appears on the left side and vice – versa. A mirror – image is therefore said to be laterally inverted and the phenomenon is called lateral inversion.

Mirror Image of Capital Letters

Letters	Mirror Image	Letters	Mirror Image	Letters	Mirror Image
A	A	J	ꞁ	S	Ƨ
B	ꓭ	K	ꓘ	T	T
C	Ɔ	L	⅃	U	U
D	ꓷ	M	M	V	V
E	Ǝ	N	И	W	W
F	ꓞ	O	O	X	X
G	ꓨ	P	ꟼ	Y	Y
H	H	Q	Ọ	Z	Ƹ
I	I	R	Я	–	–

Remark: The letters which have their mirror images identical to the letter itself are:

A, H, I, M, O, T, U, V, W, X, Y

Example: Mirror – images of certain words are given below:

1. FUN   :   ИUꟻ
2. STOP   :   ꟼOTƧ
3. ZEBRA   :   ꓯЯꓭƎƸ
4. GOLKONDA   :   ꓯꓷИOꓘ⅃Oꓨ
5. XYLOPHONE   :   ƎИOHꟼO⅃YX

Mirror Image of Small Letters

Letters	Mirror Image	Letters	Mirror Image	Letters	Mirror Image
a	ɑ	j	ꞁ	s	ƨ
b	d	k	ꓘ	t	ƚ
c	ɔ	l	l	u	ʊ
d	b	m	m	v	v
e	ɘ	n	ᴎ	w	w
f	ꟻ	o	o	x	x
g	ϱ	p	q	y	γ
h	ʜ	q	p	z	ƹ
i	i	r	ɿ		

Example: Mirror – images of certain words are given below:

1. arpit : ɟiqɿɒ
2. blade : ǝbɒld
3. determine : ǝnimɿǝʇǝb

Mirror Image of Numbers

Numbers	Mirror Image	Numbers	Mirror Image	Numbers	Mirror Image
1	I	4	４	7	７
2	２	5	５	8	8
3	３	6	６	9	９

Example: Mirror-images of certain combinations of alphabets and numbers are given below:

1. alpha348mz1 : ɪzm84Ɛɒʜqlɒ
2. BMC49JN2317 : ⱱƖƐƧИⱢ94ƆMꓭ
3. 15bg82XQh : ʜQX28ǫd2Ɩ

Direction (1 to 16): In each of the following questions, there is combination of alphabet or number followed by four alternatives. Choose the alternative which most clearly resembles the mirror image of the given combination.

1. TERMINATE
   (a) ETANIMRET (b) TERMINATE
   (c) ETANIMRET (d) ETANIMRET

2. 1965INDOPAK
   (a) KAPODNI5691 (b) PAKINDO5691
   (c) 1965INDOPAK (d) KAPODNI5691

3. NATIONAL
   (a) JANOITAN (b) JANOITAN
   (c) JANOITAN (d) LANOITAN

4. UTZFY6KH
   (a) UTZFY6KH (b) HK6YFZTU
   (c) HK6YFZTU (d) HKJYFZTU

5. SUPERVISOR
   (a) ROSIVREPUS (b) SUPERVISOR
   (c) RSOUPSERIA (d) SUPERVISOR

6. JUDGEMENT
   (a) TNEMEGDUJ (b) JUDGEMENT
   (c) TNEMEGDUJ (d) IUDGEMENT

7. ANS43Q12
   (a) ANS43Q12 (b) 21Q34SNA
   (c) 12Q34ANS (d) 12Q34SNA

8. BRISK
   (a) BRISK (b) BRISK
   (c) KSIRB (d) BRISK

9. EFFECTIVE
   (a) EVITCEFFE (b) EVITCEFFE
   (c) EVITCEFFE (d) EVITCEFFE

10. TARAIN1014A
    (a) TARAIN1014A (b) A1014NIARAT
    (c) A1014NIARAT (d) A1014NIARAT

11. MAGAZINE
    (a) MAGAZINE (b) MAGAZINE
    (c) MAGAZINE (d) MAGAZINE

12. BR4AQ16HI
    (a) BR4AQ16HI (b) IH61QA4RB
    (c) IH61QA4RB (d) IH61QA4RB

13. DL9CG4728
    (a) DL9CG4728 (b) 8274GCJD
    (c) 8274GCJD (d) 8274GCJD

14. IMFORMATIONS
    (a) INFORMATIONS (b) INFORMATIONS
    (c) INFORMATIONS (d) INFORMATIONS

15. REASONING
    (a) REASONING (b) REASONING
    (c) REASONING (d) REASONING

16. AN54WMG3
    (a) AN54WMG3 (b) 3GMW45NA
    (c) 3GMW45NA (d) 3GMW45NA

Direction (17 to 30): In each of the following questions, choose the correct mirror image of the figure (X) from amongst the four alternatives (a), (b), (c) and (d) given along with Fig. (X).

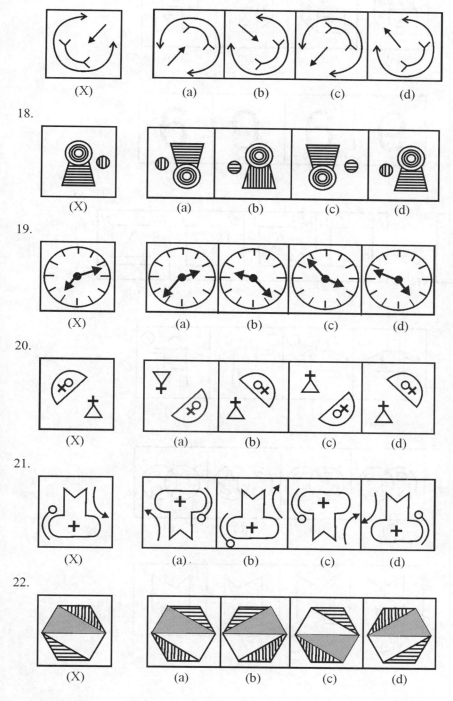

17.

   (X)   (a)   (b)   (c)   (d)

18.

   (X)   (a)   (b)   (c)   (d)

19.

   (X)   (a)   (b)   (c)   (d)

20.

   (X)   (a)   (b)   (c)   (d)

21.

   (X)   (a)   (b)   (c)   (d)

22.

   (X)   (a)   (b)   (c)   (d)

23.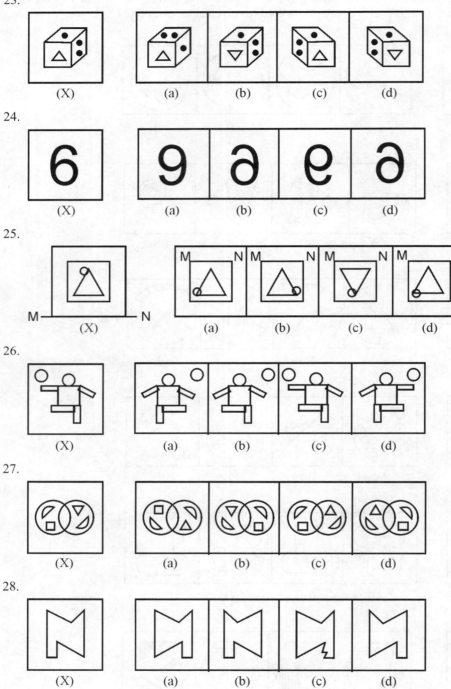

24.

25.

26.

27.

28.

29.

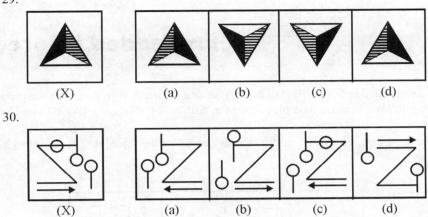

(X) (a) (b) (c) (d)

30.

(X) (a) (b) (c) (d)

Embedded Figure

A figure (A) is said to be embedded in figure (B) if figure (B) contains figure A as its parts. In such problems a figure (A) is given, followed by four complex figures in such a way that figure (A) is embedded in one and only one of them.

In these questions, the candidate has to analyze the figures and select the figure in which figure (X) is embedded.

Example 1:

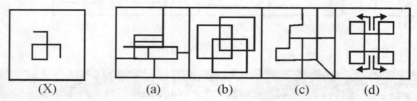

Solution: (b)

Direction (1 to 30): Analyze the set of figures and choose the correct option that contains figure X.

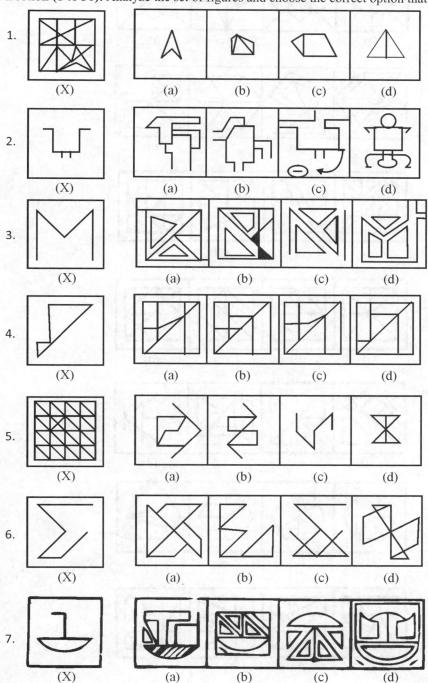

1. (X) (a) (b) (c) (d)

2. (X) (a) (b) (c) (d)

3. (X) (a) (b) (c) (d)

4. (X) (a) (b) (c) (d)

5. (X) (a) (b) (c) (d)

6. (X) (a) (b) (c) (d)

7. (X) (a) (b) (c) (d)

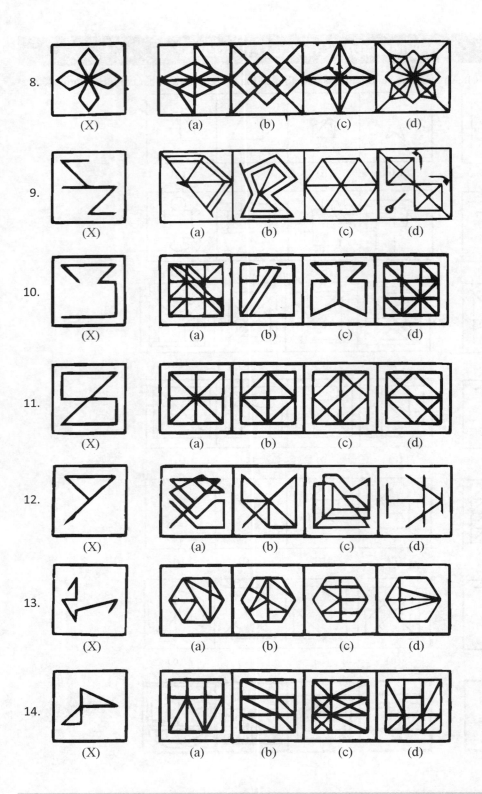

8. (X)   (a)   (b)   (c)   (d)

9. (X)   (a)   (b)   (c)   (d)

10. (X)   (a)   (b)   (c)   (d)

11. (X)   (a)   (b)   (c)   (d)

12. (X)   (a)   (b)   (c)   (d)

13. (X)   (a)   (b)   (c)   (d)

14. (X)   (a)   (b)   (c)   (d)

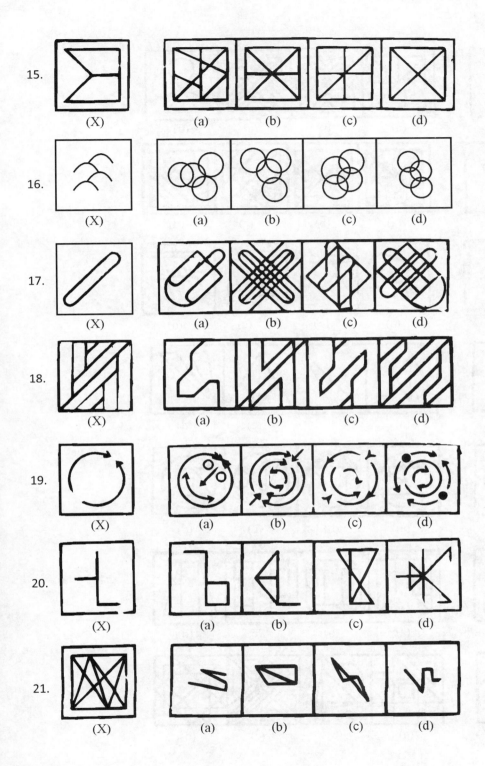

15. (X)   (a)   (b)   (c)   (d)

16. (X)   (a)   (b)   (c)   (d)

17. (X)   (a)   (b)   (c)   (d)

18. (X)   (a)   (b)   (c)   (d)

19. (X)   (a)   (b)   (c)   (d)

20. (X)   (a)   (b)   (c)   (d)

21. (X)   (a)   (b)   (c)   (d)

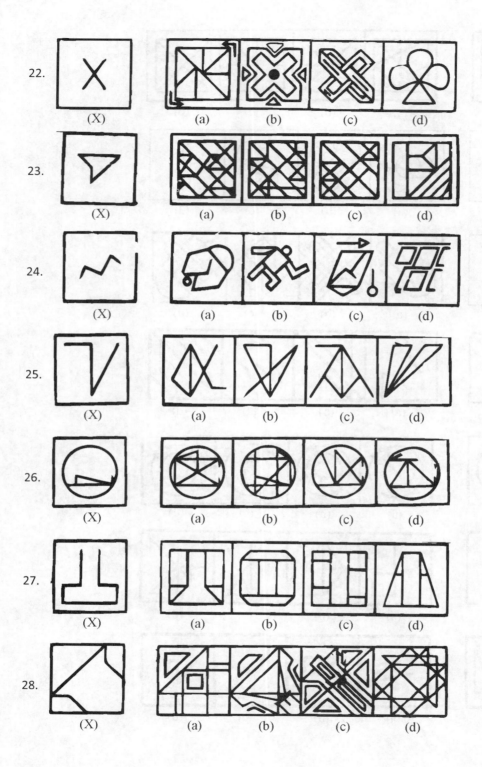

22. (X) (a) (b) (c) (d)

23. (X) (a) (b) (c) (d)

24. (X) (a) (b) (c) (d)

25. (X) (a) (b) (c) (d)

26. (X) (a) (b) (c) (d)

27. (X) (a) (b) (c) (d)

28. (X) (a) (b) (c) (d)

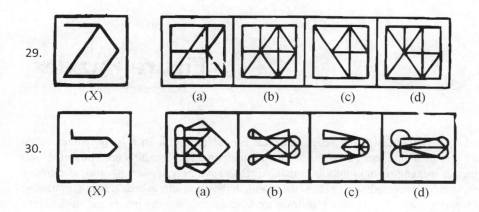

29.

(X)   (a)   (b)   (c)   (d)

30.

(X)   (a)   (b)   (c)   (d)

Answer Key

1. (c)	2. (d)	3. (a)	4. (d)	5. (c)	6. (c)	7. (b)	8. (d)	9. (d)	10. (a)
11. (a)	12. (a)	13. (d)	14. (c)	15. (b)	16. (c)	17. (b)	18. (c)	19. (a)	20. (b)
21. (a)	22. (d)	23. (a)	24. (b)	25. (b)	26. (b)	27. (a)	28. (d)	29. (b)	30. (b)

The questions based on Figure Puzzles are designed to test candidate's skills in solving mathematical operations and numbers. In mathematical operations, usual mathematical symbols are converted into another form by either interchanging the symbols or using different symbols in place of original symbols in order to make simple calculation tedious. On the other hand, in the questions asked on number puzzles, a few numbers are inserted into a figure which follows a particular rule for the placement of different numbers at different places. Students are asked to select the missing number, following the rule of placement of numbers, from the given options.

Example 1:

Which number will replace the question mark?

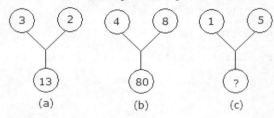

Solution:

From figure a: $(3)^2 + (2)^2 = 13$
From figure b: $(4)^2 + (8)^2 = 80$
From figure c: $? = (1)^2 + (5)^2$
             $= 1 + 25$
             $= 26$

Hence the number 26 will replace the question mark.

Example 2:

Which number will replace the question mark?

9	17	16
5	4	?
5	4	8
9	17	8

Solution:

From column I: $(9 \times 5) \div 5 = 9$

From column II: $(17 \times 4) \div 4 = 17$

From column III: $(16 \times ?) \div 8 = 8$

$$16 \times ? = 64$$
$$\Rightarrow \quad ? = 4$$

Hence the number 4 will replace the question mark.

Example 3:

Which number will replace the question mark?

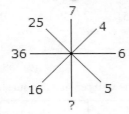

Solution: Here,
$$(5)^2 = 25$$
$$(6)^2 = 36$$
$$(4)^2 = 16$$
$$\therefore \ (7)^2 = 49$$

Hence, the number 49 will replace the question mark.

Direction (1 to 25):

In this type of questions, a figure or a matrix is given in which some numbers are filled according to a rule. A place is left blank. You have to find out a character (a number or a letter) from the given possible answers which may be filled in the blank space.

1. Which one will replace the question mark?

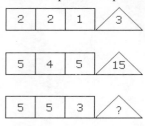

(a) 11   (b) 19
(c) 15   (d) 22

2. Which one will replace the question mark?

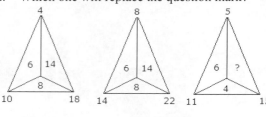

(a) 8   (b) 14
(c) 10   (d) 6

3. Which one will replace the question mark?

(a) 80   (b) 114
(c) 108   (d) None of these

4. Which one will replace the question mark?

(a) 18   (b) 20
(c) 21   (d) 19

5. Which one will replace the question mark?
(a) 660   (b) 670

(c) 610   (d) 690

6. Which one will replace the question mark?

3	6	8
5	8	4
4	7	?

(a) 6   (b) 7
(c) 8   (d) 9

7. Which one will replace the question mark?

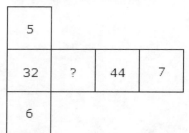

(a) 33   (b) 38
(c) 32   (d) 37

8. Which one will replace the question mark?

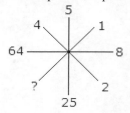

(a) 1   (b) 2
(c) 3   (d) 4

9. Which one will replace the question mark?

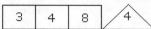

(a) 8   (b) 9
(c) 10   (d) 11

10. Which one will replace the question mark?

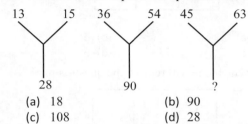

(a) 18   (b) 90
(c) 108   (d) 28

11. Which one will replace the question mark?

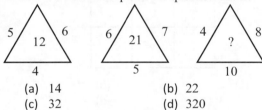

(a) 14   (b) 22
(c) 32   (d) 320

12. Which one will replace the question mark?

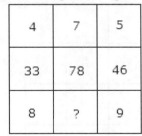

(a) 12   (b) 13
(c) 11   (d) 10

13. Which one will replace the question mark?

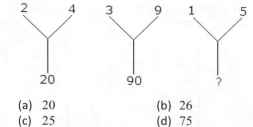

(a) 20   (b) 26
(c) 25   (d) 75

14. Which one will replace the question mark?

3	?	5
5	4	7
4	4	4
60	96	140

(a) 4   (b) 6
(c) 9   (d) 8

15. Which one will replace the question mark?

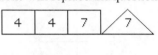

(a) 2   (b) 4
(c) 6   (d) 8

16. Which one will replace the question mark?

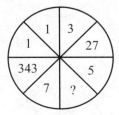

(a) 25   (b) 625
(c) 125   (d) 50

17. Which one will replace the question mark?

4	9	2
3	5	7
8	1	?

(a) 9   (b) 6
(c) 15   (d) 14

18. Which one will replace the question mark?

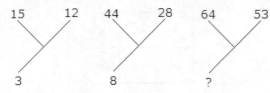

(a) 30   (b) 13
(c) 70   (d) 118

19. Which one will replace the question mark?

(a) 40   (b) 38
(c) 44   (d) 39

20. Which one will replace the question mark?

(a) 60   (b) 46
(c) 86   (d) 75

21. Which one will replace the question mark?

(a) 3   (b) 2
(c) 7   (d) 6

22. Which one will replace the question mark?

5	6	5
8	9	7
10	7	?
400	378	315

(a) 9   (b) 5
(c) 7   (d) 3

23. Which one will replace the question mark?

1	$\frac{1}{2}$	$\frac{3}{2}$
2	$\frac{2}{3}$	$\frac{8}{3}$
3	?	$\frac{19}{5}$

(a) 1/2   (b) 2/3
(c) 3/4   (d) 4/5

24. Which one will replace the question mark?

7	4	5
8	7	6
3	3	?
29	19	31

(a) 3   (b) 5
(c) 4   (d) 6

25. Which one will replace the question mark?

4	5	6
2	3	7
1	8	3
21	98	?

(a) 94   (b) 76
(c) 16   (d) 73

Answer Key

1. (d)	2. (c)	3. (c)	4. (b)	5. (d)	6. (a)	7. (d)	8. (a)
9. (d)	10. (c)	11. (c)	12. (c)	13. (b)	14. (b)	15. (c)	16. (c)
17. (b)	18. (b)	19. (b)	20. (c)	21. (b)	22. (a)	23. (d)	24. (b)
25. (a)							

Hints and Solutions

1. **(d)**
   From figure I $(2 \times 2 - 1) = 3$
   and from figure II $(5 \times 4 - 5) = 15$
   From figure III $(5 \times 5 - 3) = 22$

2. **(c)**
   For first triangle,
   $10 - 4 = 6$
   $18 - 10 = 8$
   $18 - 4 = 14$
   For second triangle,
   $14 - 8 = 6$
   $22 - 14 = 8$
   $22 - 8 = 14$
   For third triangle,
   $11 - 5 = 6$
   $15 - 11 = 4$
   $\therefore ? = 15 - 5 = 10$

3. **(c)**
   From figure I $(4 + 8) \times 9 = 108$
   $\therefore ? = (5 + 4) \times 12 = 108$

4. **(b)**
   $1 + 2 + 3 + 4 = 10$
   and $1 + 3 + 5 + 8 = 17$
   Similarly, $? = 1 + 4 + 6 + 9 = 20$

5. **(d)**
   From figure I $(1)^2 + (5)^2 + (4)^2 + (3)^2$
   $= 51 \times 10 = 510$
   and from figure II $(3)^2 + (4)^2 + (6)^2 + (2)^2$
   $= 65 \times 10 = 650$
   Similarly, from figure III $(0)^2 + (1)^2 + (2)^2 + (8)^2 = 69 \times 10 = 690$

6. **(a)**
   From column I $(5 + 3)/2 = 4$
   and From column II $(6 + 8)/2 = 7$
   Therefore from column III $? = (8 + 4)/2 = 6$

7. **(d)** Here,
   $(5 \times 6) + 2 = 32$
   $(7 \times 6) + 2 = 44$
   $\therefore ? = (7 \times 5) + 2 = 37$

8. **(a)** Here,
   $(2)^2 = 4$
   $(8)^2 = 64$
   $(5)^2 = 25$
   $\therefore ? = (1)^2 = 1$

9. **(d)**
   From figure I $(3 \times 4 - 8) = 4$
   From figure II $(2 \times 5 - 4) = 6$
   and from figure III $(4 \times 5 - 9) = 11$

10. **(c)**
    From figure I $13 + 15 = 28$
    From figure II $36 + 54 = 90$
    Therefore, from figure III $45 + 63 = 108$

11. **(c)**
    From figure I $(5 \times 6 \times 4)/10 = 12$
    and from figure II $(6 \times 7 \times 5)/10 = 21$
    Therefore, from figure III $? =$
    $(4 \times 8 \times 10)/10 = 32$

12. **(c)**
    From column I $(4 \times 8) + 1 = 33$
    From column II $(5 \times 9) + 1 = 46$
    Similarly, from column III $(7 \times ?) + 1$
    $= 78$
    $? = \dfrac{77}{7} = 11$

13. **(b)**
    $(2)^2 + (4)^2 = 20$
    $(3)^2 + (9)^2 = 90$
    Therefore, $? = (1)^2 + (5)^2 = 26$

14. **(b)**
    $3 \times 5 \times 4 = 60$
    and $5 \times 7 \times 4 = 140$
    Therefore, $4 \times 4 \times ? = 96$
    $\Rightarrow ? = (96/16) = 6$

15. **(c)**
    $(4 \times 7) \div 4 = 7$
    and $(6 \times 2) \div 3 = 4$
    Therefore, $(6 \times 2) \div 2 = 6$

16. **(c)**

All numbers are cubes,

$(7)^3 = 343$

$(1)^3 = 1$

$(3)^3 = 27$

Similarly, $? = (5)^3 = 125$

17. **(b)** Here,

$(4 + 9 + 2) = (3 + 5 + 7) = (8 + 1 + ?)$

$\Rightarrow ? = 15 - 9 = 6$

Total in each case = 15

18. **(b)**

$(15 + 12)/9 = 3$

and $(44 + 28)/9 = 8$

Therefore, $? = (64 + 53)/9 = \dfrac{117}{9} = 13$

19. **(b)** Here,

$9 + (2)^2 = 13$

and $13 + (3)^2 = 22$

and $? = 22 + (4)^2 = 38$

20. **(c)**

$(30 - 24) \times 8 = 48$

and $(23 - 12) \times 8 = 88$

Therefore, $(92 - ?) \times 8 = 48$

$\Rightarrow 92 - ? = 6$

$\Rightarrow \qquad ? = 92 - 6 = 86$

21. **(b)**

Putting the position of the letters in reverse order

P = 11, S = 8, V = 5 and Y = 2

22. **(a)**

From column I $5 \times 8 \times 10 = 400$

and from column II $6 \times 9 \times 7 = 378$

Therefore from column III $5 \times 7 \times ?$

$= 315$

$? = 9$

23. **(d)**

From I row, $1 + (1/2) = 3/2$

From II row, $2 + (2/3) = 8/3$

From III row, $3 + ? = 19/5$

$? = (19/5) - 3$

$? = (4/5)$

24. **(b)**

From column I $(7 \times 3) + 8 = 29$

From column II $(4 \times 3) + 7 = 19$

From column III $(5 \times ?) + 6 = 31$

$? = 5.$

25. **(a)**

From column I $(4)^2 + (2)^2 + (1)^2 = 21$

and from column II $(5)^2 + (3)^2 + (8)^2 = 98$

Therefore from column III

$(6)^2 + (7)^2 + (3)^2 = 94$

Section 3

ACHIEVERS SECTION

High Order Thinking Skills (HOTS)

Multiple Choice Questions

1. What is the smallest number which when diminished by 7 is divisible by 21, 28, 36 & 45?

   (a) 1260   (b) 1263

   (c) 1267   (d) 1253

2. A car moves at a uniform speed of 65 km per hour. How much distance it will cover in 25 hours?

   (a) 1525 km   (b) 1625 km

   (c) 1675 km   (d) 1645 km

3. What is the product of sum and difference of largest 3-digit number and smallest 3-digit number?

   (a) 988001   (b) 98801

   (c) 988011   (d) None of these

4. What fraction of an hour is 12 minutes?

   (a) $\dfrac{1}{5}$ (b) $\dfrac{1}{3}$

   (c) $\dfrac{1}{6}$ (d) $\dfrac{2}{5}$

5. What must be subtracted from $a^3 - 4a^2 + 7a - 6$ to obtain $a^2 - 5a + 2$?

   (a) $a^3 - 5a^2 + 12a - 8$

   (b) $a^3 - 4a^2 + 2a + 8$

   (c) $a^3 - 5a^2 - 12a + 8$

   (d) None of these

6. A factory produces electric bulbs. If 2 out of every 10 bulbs is defective. The factory produces 820 bulbs per day. What are the number of defective bulbs produced each day?

   (a) 82   (b) 84

   (c) 164   (d) 168

7. In covering 111 km, a car consumes 6 L of petrol. How many kilometers will it go in 15 L of petrol?

   (a) 257.5 km   (b) 265 km

   (c) 271.5 km   (d) 277.5 km

8. If there are 72 spokes in a bicycle wheel, then the angle between a pain of adjacent spokes is

   (a) 5°   (b) 10°

   (c) 12°   (d) 15°

9. The measure of two angles of a triangle are 67° and 43°. What is the measure of third angle?

   (a) 60°   (b) 65°

   (c) 70°   (d) 80°

10. In an isosceles $\triangle ABC$, the bisector of $\angle B$ and $\angle C$ meet at a point O. If $\angle A = 80°$ then what is the measure of $\angle BOC$?

    (a) 80°   (b) 130°

    (c) 100°   (d) 120°

11. If the diagonals of a quadrilateral bisect each other at right angle then the quadrilateral is a

    (a) Rhombus   (b) Rectangle

    (c) Kite   (d) None of these

12. The cost of fencing a square field at Rs. 35 per meter is Rs. 4480. What is area of the field?

    (a) 864 m^2 (b) 964 m^2

    (c) 984 m^2 (d) 1024 m^2

13. The diameter of a wheel of a car is 70 cm. How many revolutions will it make to travel 1.65 km?

(a) 650   (b) 750

(c) 800   (d) 850

14. What is the value of x in the given figure if l 11m.

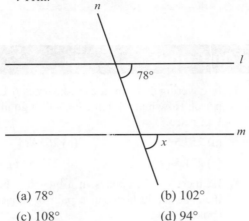

(a) 78°   (b) 102°

(c) 108°   (d) 94°

15. If 15 tins of same size contains. 234 kg of oil. How much oil will there be in 20 such tins?

(a) 292 kg   (b) 302 kg

(c) 312 kg   (d) 322 kg

16. The mass of a brick is 3 kg 225 g. What is the total mass of 37 such bricks?

(a) 117.325 kg   (b) 119.325 kg

(c) 118.325 kg   (d) 121.325 kg

17. What is the sum of XLVI and XCIX?

(a) 142   (b) 143

(c) 144   (d) 145

18. What is the sum of first five prime numbers which are greater than 100?

(a) 531   (b) 528

(c) 529   (d) 533

19. What is the greatest number which divides 285 and 1249 leaving remainder 9 and 7 respectively?

(a) 134   (b) 136

(c) 138   (d) 142

20. What is the least number which is divisible by 2, 3, 7, 12, 16, 18 and 30?

21. If 5 is subtracted from three times a number the result is 16. What is the number?

(a) 7   (b) 8

(c) 9   (d) 11

22. What is the share of B if Rs. 6900 is divided among A, B & C in the ratio 3 : 5 : 7?

(a) 2100   (b) 2300

(c) 2350   (d) 2400

23. The ratio of income to expenditure of Mohan is 7 : 5. What is the saving if the income is 14000?

(a) Rs. 4000   (b) Rs. 4200

(c) Rs. 4500   (d) 4600

24. What is the value of x if $16(3x - 5) - 10(4x - 8) = 40$

(a) 4   (b) 5

(c) 7   (d) 10

25. The radius of a pencil is 6 mm and its length is 15 cm. What is the ratio of diameter of the pencil to the length of the pencil?

(a) 2 : 25   (b) 1 : 25

(c) 3 : 25   (d) 4 : 25

26. If HCF and LCM of two numbers are 131 and 8253. One of the number is 917. What is the other?

(a) 1149   (b) 1159

(c) 1169   (d) 1179

27. What is the difference between place value and face value of 7 in 7063?

(a) 6993   (b) 6399

(c) 6939   (d) None of these

28. What is the smallest 5-digit number divisible by 111?

(a) 10011   (b) 10101

(c) 10111   (d) 10110

29. What is the least number of 5-digits that is exactly divisible by 16, 18, 24 & 30?

(a) 10020   (b) 10040

(c) 10080   (d) 10200

30. What is the value of 1 + 0.1 + 0.001?

(a) 1.010   (b) 1.111

(c) 1.011   (d) None of these

31. $0.213 \div 0.00213 = ?$

(a) 10   (b) 100

(c) 1000   (d) $\dfrac{1}{10}$

32. What is the value of x if

$$\dfrac{144}{0.144} = \dfrac{14.4}{x} \ ?$$

(a) 0.144   (b) 1.44

(c) 0.0144   (d) None of these

33. What is the largest number of 4-digit exactly divisible by 12, 15, 18 & 27?

(a) 9900   (b) 9909

(c) 9990   (d) None of these

34. What is difference between two right angles and two straight angles?

(a) 0°   (b) 90°

(c) 180º   (d) 360°

35. What is the value of P if

$$\dfrac{P-3}{2} - 5 = \dfrac{P-1}{3} + 7$$

(a) 59   (b) 69

(c) 79   (d) 89

36. $5\dfrac{1}{2} - 3\dfrac{2}{3} + 7\dfrac{1}{5} - 6\dfrac{1}{4} = ?$

(a) $3\dfrac{17}{60}$ (b) $2\dfrac{47}{60}$

(c) $2\dfrac{57}{60}$ (d) $2\dfrac{41}{60}$

37. What is the wrong number in the given sequence

1, 8, 27, 64, 124, 216, 343

(a) 45   (b) 46

(c) 47   (d) 48

39. Which is the largest fraction among

$\dfrac{4}{7}, \dfrac{2}{3}, \dfrac{1}{8}, \dfrac{5}{6}, \dfrac{7}{9} \ ?$

(a) $\dfrac{7}{9}$ (b) $\dfrac{5}{6}$

(c) $\dfrac{4}{7}$ (d) $\dfrac{2}{3}$

40. What will be the least number which when doubled will be exactly divisible by 12, 18, 21 & 30?

(a) 630   (b) 640

(c) 660   (d) 680

Answer Key

1. (c)	2. (b)	3. (a)	4. (a)	5. (a)	6. (c)	7. (d)	8. (a)	9. (c)	10 (b)
11. (a)	12. (d)	13. (b)	14. (a)	15. (c)	16. (b)	17. (d)	18. (a)	19. (c)	20. (c)
21. (a)	22. (b)	23. (a)	24. (b)	25. (a)	26. (d)	27. (a)	28. (b)	29. (c)	30. (b)
31. (b)	32. (c)	33. (a)	34. (c)	35. (c)	36. (b)	37. (a)	38. (b)	39. (b)	40. (a)

Hints and Solutions

1. (c)

LCM of 21, 28, 36, 45 = 1260

Required Number = 1260 + 7 = 1267

2. (b)

Distance = Speed × Time = 65 × 25 = 1625 km

3. (a)

Largest 3-digit number = 999

Smallest 3-digit number = 100

Sum = 999 + 100 = 1099

Difference = 999 − 100 = 899

Product = 1099 × 899 = 988001

4. (a)

Required fraction = $\dfrac{12\,\text{minutes}}{60\,\text{minutes}} = \dfrac{1}{5}$

5. (a)

$(a^3 - 4a^2 + 7a - 6) - K = a^2 - 5a + 2$

$K = a^3 - 4a^2 + 7a - 6 - a^2 - 5a - 2$

$a^3 - 5a^2 + 12a - 8$

6. (c)

$\dfrac{\text{Defective bulbs}}{\text{Total bulbs}} = \dfrac{2}{10} = \dfrac{x}{820}$

$x = \dfrac{2 \times 820}{10} = 164$

7. (d)

Required distance = $\dfrac{111 \times 15}{6} = 277.5\,\text{km}$

8. (a)

Angle = $\dfrac{360°}{72} = 5°$

9. (c)

Third angle = $180° - (67° + 43°) = 70°$

10. (b)

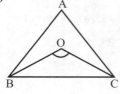

11.

∠A = 80°

∠B + ∠C = 180° − 80° = 100°

$\dfrac{1}{2}(∠B + ∠C) = \dfrac{100°}{2} = 50°;$

∠BOC = 180° − 50° = 130°

12. (d)

Perimeter of square field = $\dfrac{4480}{35} = 128$

4 × side = 128 ⇒ side = 32 m

Area = $(32)^2 = 1024\,\text{m}^2$

13. (b)

Circumference = $\pi d = \dfrac{22}{7} \times 70 = 220\,\text{cm}$

Number of revolution = $\dfrac{1.65 \times 1000 \times 100}{220}$

$= \dfrac{165 \times 1000}{220} = 750$

14. (a)

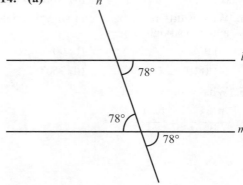

$x = 78°$ as $l \parallel m$

15. (c)

$\dfrac{234 \times 20}{15} = 312\,\text{kg}$

16. (b)

Mass of 37 bricks = 3.225 × 37

= 119.325 kg

17. (d)

XLVI = XL + VI = (50 − 10) + (5 + 1) = 46

XCIX = (100 − 10) + (10 − 1) = 90 + 9 = 99

Sum = 46 + 99 = 145

18. (a)

Sum = 101 + 103 + 107 + 109 + 111 = 531

19. (c)

285 − 9 = 276; 1249 − 7 = 1242

HCF of 276 and 1242 = 138

20. (c)

LCM of 2, 3, 7, 12, 16, 18, 30 = 5040

21. (a)

Let the number be x

$3x − 5 = 16$

$3x = 21 \Rightarrow x = \dfrac{21}{3} = 7$

22. (b)

Share of B = $\dfrac{5}{(3+5+7)} \times 6900$

$= 2300$

23. (a)

Saving = 7 − 5 = 2

$\dfrac{2}{7} = \dfrac{x}{14000} \Rightarrow x = \dfrac{2 \times 14000}{7} = 4000$

24. (b)

$16(3x − 5) − 10(4x − 8) = 40$

$48x − 80 − 40x + 80 = 40$

$8x = 40 \Rightarrow x = \dfrac{40}{8} = 5$

25. (a)

Diameter of the pencil = 6 × 2 = 12 mm

Required ratio = $\dfrac{12\,\text{mm}}{15 \times 10\,\text{mm}} = \dfrac{2}{25} = 2 : 25$

26. (d)

Other number = $\dfrac{131 \times 8253}{917} = 1179$

27. (a)

Difference = 7000 − 7 = 6993

28. (b)

Smallest five digit number = 10000

Required number = 10000 + (111 − 10)

= 10101

29. (c)

LCM of 16, 18, 24, 30 = 1440

Smallest 5-digit number = 10000

Required number = 10000 + (1440 − 1360)

= 10080

30. (b)

1 + 0.1 + 0.01 + 0.001 = 1.111

31. (b)

0. 213 ÷ 0.00213

$= \dfrac{213}{1000} \div \dfrac{213}{100000} = \dfrac{213}{1000} \times \dfrac{100000}{213} = 100$

32. (c)

$\dfrac{144}{0.144} = \dfrac{14.4}{x}$

$x = \dfrac{0.144 \times 14.4}{144} = \dfrac{144 \times 144}{144 \times 1000 \times 10}$

$= \dfrac{144}{10000} = 0.0144$

33. (a)

LCM of 12, 15, 18, 27 = 180

Largest number of 4-digit = 9999

Required number = 9999 − 99 = 9900

34. (c)

Two right angles = 2 × 90° = 180°

Two straight angles = 2 × 180° = 360°

Difference = 360° − 180° = 180°

35. (c)

$\dfrac{P-3}{2} − 5 = \dfrac{P-1}{3} + 7$

$$\frac{P-3-10}{2}=\frac{P-1+21}{3}$$

$$\frac{P-13}{2}=\frac{P+20}{3}$$

$3P - 39 = 2P + 40$

$3P - 2P = 40 + 39$

$P = 79$

36. (b)

$$5\frac{1}{2}-3\frac{2}{3}+7\frac{1}{5}-6\frac{1}{4}$$

$$\frac{11}{2}-\frac{11}{3}+\frac{36}{5}-\frac{25}{4}=\frac{330-220+432-375}{60}$$

$$=\frac{762-595}{60}=\frac{167}{60}=2\frac{47}{60}$$

37. (a)

1,	8,	27,	64,	124,	216,	343
↓	↓	↓	↓	↓	↓	↓
1^3	2^3	3^3	4^3	5^3	6^3	7^3

38. (b)

8	13	21	32,	46	63,	83
	+5	+8	+11	+14	+17	+20

39. (b)

LCM of 7, 3, 8, 6, 9 = 504

$$\frac{4}{7}=\frac{4\times72}{7\times72}=\frac{288}{504};\frac{2}{3}=\frac{2\times168}{3\times168}=\frac{336}{504}$$

$$\frac{1}{8}=\frac{1\times63}{8\times63}=\frac{63}{504};\frac{5}{6}=\frac{5\times84}{6\times84}=\frac{420}{504}$$

$$\frac{7}{9}=\frac{7\times56}{9\times56}=\frac{392}{504}$$

$\frac{5}{6}$ is largest

40. (a)

LCM of 12, 18, 21, 30 = 1260

Required number = $1260 \div 2 = 630$

Section 4
SUBJECTIVE QUESTIONS

Short Answer Questions

1. A shopkeeper has 500kg of sugar. He sells 45kg sugar on each day. How much sugar was left after the sale of 8 days?

2. If a milk booth sells 223 litres of milk every day. Find the total quantity of milk sold by the both in the month of February 2006?

3. Sunil multiplied 2356 by 54 instead of multiplying by 45. By how much was his answer greater than the correct answer?

4. What is the Hindu – Arabic numeral of the Roman numeral CCCLIX?

5. Find the sum and difference of face value and place value of 7 in the number 62714.

6. What is the difference between largest four digit number and smallest five digit number?

7. On dividing 535 by 31, the remainder is 8 then what is the quotient?

8. What is the least 4-digit number that is exactly divisible by 14?

9. What is the largest 4 – digit number that is divisible by 17?

10. What is the predecessor of smallest 4 – digit number?

11. Find the smallest number having four different prime factors.

12. What is the longest tape that can be used by measure exactly the lengths 84cm, 1m 38cm and 12m?

13. Four bells toll at intervals of 4, 7, 12 & 84 seconds. The bells toll together at 5 o'clock. How many times will they do so in 28 minutes?

14. Find the greatest number of 4 – digits which is exactly divisible by 12, 16, 28 and 36.

15. Raju painted $\frac{2}{7}$ of the wall in his room. Rakesh painted $\frac{4}{7}$ of the wall. How much did they paint together? How much wall is stoll left unpainted?

16. A container has 726.94 litres of oil. Two drums of capacity 142.6 litres and 106.8 litres are filled from the container. What is the quantity of oil left in the container?

17. What is the difference in perimeters of equilateral triangle and hexagon having side 7 cm?

18. What is the area of square whose perimeter is 84cm?

19. Find the number of square tiles of size 15cm required for covering the floor of a room 9m long and 6m wide.

20. Five square pieces each of side 3cm are cut from a rectangular board 9cm long and 7cm wide. What is the area of remaining part of the board?

Hints *and* Solutions

1. Required sugar = $500 - (45 \times 8)$
   $$= 500 - 360 = 140 \text{ kg}$$

2. Quantity of milk = $223 \times 28 = 6244$

3. $2356 \times (54 - 45) = 2356 \times 9 = 21204$

4. We have
   $$CCCLIX = 100 + 100 + 100 + 50 + 9 = 359$$

5. If x is the quotient then
   Sum = $7 + 700 = 707$
   Difference = $700 - 7 = 693$

6. Difference = $10000 - 9999 = 1$

7. $31 \times x + 8 = 535$
   $$\Rightarrow 31x = 535 - 8 \Rightarrow 31x = 527$$
   $$\Rightarrow x = \frac{527}{31} = 17$$

8. Required least 4 digit number
   $$= 1000 - 6 + 14 = 1008$$

9. Required largest 4 digit number
   $$= 9999 - 3 = 9996$$

10. Smallest 4 – digit number = 1000
    Predecessor = $1000 - 1 = 999$

11. Required smallest number =
    $2 \times 3 \times 5 \times 7 = 210$

12. HCF of 84 cm, 138 cm & 1200 cm = 6 cm

13. LCM of 4, 7, 12, 84 = 84.
    No. of times the bells will toll together in 28
    minutes = $\dfrac{28 \times 60}{84} = 20$

15. Total painted wall = $\dfrac{2}{7} + \dfrac{4}{7} = \dfrac{2+4}{7} = \dfrac{6}{7}$

    The wall left unpainted = $1 - \dfrac{6}{7} = \dfrac{7-6}{7} = \dfrac{1}{7}$

16. Oil left in the container
    $$= 726.94 - (142.6 + 106.8)$$
    $$= 726.94 - 249.4$$
    $$= 477.54 \text{ litres}$$

17. Perimeter of hexagon = $6 \times 7 = 42$ cm
    Perimeter of equilateral triangle = 3×7
    $$= 21 \text{ cm}$$
    Difference = $42 - 21 = 21$ cm

18. Perimeter of square = 84
    $$\Rightarrow \qquad 4 \times \text{side} = 84$$
    $$\Rightarrow \qquad \text{side} = \frac{84}{4} = 21 \text{ cm}$$
    $\therefore$ Area of square = $(21)^2 = 441 \text{ cm}^2$

19. No. of square tiles = $\dfrac{9\,\text{m} \times 6\,\text{m}}{15\,\text{cm}}$
    $$= \frac{9 \times 100 \times 6 \times 100}{15}$$
    $$= 3600$$

20. Area of remaining part of the board
    $$= 9 \times 7 - (3 \times 3 \times 5)$$
    $$= 63 - 45 = 18 \text{ cm}^2$$

Section 5
MODEL PAPERS

1. If white is red, red is yellow, is orange, orange is blue, blue is violet, violet is green, then what is the colour of brinjal?

   (a) Violet   (b) Blue

   (c) Green   (d) Yellow

2. If LAPTOP is written as NYRROQN then MOUSE is written as

   (a) OMVQG   (b) OMWQS
   (c) OMWPG   (d) ONWPG

3. If DELHI is coded as 451289 then what is the code for MUMBAI?

   (a) 132113219   (b) 132113318
   (c) 122112219   (d) 132013219

4. In the given sequence of numbers, how many times the number 7 is preceded by 3 and followed by 8?

   38237283337828378773787382?

   (a) 1   (b) 2
   (c) 3   (d) 4

5. In a class of 35 students Kartik is placed 7th from the bottom whereas Mohit is placed 9th from the top. Sonal is placed exactly in between Kartik and Mohit. What is Kartik's position from Sonal?

   (a) 9th   (b) 10th
   (c) 11th   (d) 8th

6. Pointing to a Photograph Arun said, she is the mother of my brother's son's wife daughter. How is the lady related to Arun.

   (a) Cousin   (b) Daughter in Law
   (c) Uncle   (d) Brother in Law

7. Choose the odd one out from the following.

   (a) 29(96)17   (b) 42(120)27
   (c) 77(76)68   (d) 64(88)53

8. Choose the odd one from the given group.

   (a) Harbour   (b) Coast
   (c) Oasis   (d) Island

9. Choose the odd numeral group

   (a) 1427   (b) 3148
   (c) 5207   (d) 3427

10. Manish walks 10m towards East and 20m towards South and 10m towards West. What distance and in which direction is to be now from starting position?

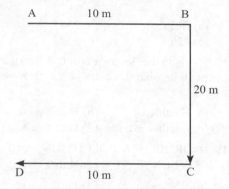

   (a) 20m North   (b) 20m South
   (c) 20m West   (d) 20m East

11. If X means +, Y means '—', Z means ÷ and P means '×' then what is the value of 10P2×5Y5?

   (a) 12   (b) 20
   (c) 65   (d) 30

12. How many 7's are there in the given sequence which are in between 2 and 5?

   82375642758275968257

   (a) 1   (b) 2
   (c) 3   (d) 4

13. If 5(16)3; 7(24)5 then 9(?)6

    (a) 43   (b) 44
    (c) 45   (d) 46

14. 17, 23, 29, 35 ?

    (a) 40   (b) 41
    (c) 42   (d) 43

15. If MAT = 34, DO = 19 then what is for MANGO?

    (a) 47   (b) 48
    (c) 49   (d) 50

16. X is the wife of 'Y' and "Y' is the brother of 'Z', 'Z' is the son of 'P'. How 'P' related to 'X'.

    (a) Sister   (b) Brother
    (c) Father-in-Law   (d) Aunt

17. If 213 = 419; 322 = 924; 415 = 16125 then 215 = ?

    (a) 4125   (b) 2541
    (c) 425   (d) 1625

18. If A is to the South of B and C is to the East of B, in what direction is A with respect to C?

    (a) North-east   (b) North-west
    (c) South-west   (d) South-east

19. If DRINK = 6 POLLUTION = 10, then GOVERNMENT is equal to?

    (a) 12   (b) 11
    (c) 10   (d) 8

20. moon : satellite : : Earth : ?

    (a) Planet   (b) Sun
    (c) Solar System   (d) Asteroid

21. Choose the word which is the least like the other words in the group

    (a) Copper   (b) Brass
    (c) Zinc   (d) Aluminium

22. Complete the series 13, 24, 46, 90, 178 …………..

    (a) 354   (b) 266
    (c) 364   (d) 344

23. Bihar is related to India in the same was as Florida is related to…………..?

    (a) Canada   (b) North America
    (c) Mexico   (d) USA

24. If in a certain language, GRASP is coded as BMVNK, which word would be coded as CRANE

    (a) GVERI   (b) HWFST
    (c) EUDQH   (d) XMVIZ

25. Raman is 7 ranks ahead of Suman in a class of 39. If Suman's rank is seventeenth from the last. What is Raman's rank from the start?

    (a) 14th   (b) 15th
    (c) 16th   (d) 17th

26. Which is the largest of the fraction

$$\frac{2}{5}, \frac{4}{7}, \frac{3}{5}, \frac{6}{7}?$$

    (a) $\dfrac{2}{5}$ (b) $\dfrac{3}{5}$

    (c) $\dfrac{4}{7}$ (d) $\dfrac{6}{7}$

27. What is the value of x if $\dfrac{1}{2}x + 7 =$

    (a) 5   (b) 12
    (c) 18   (d) 24

28. Two numbers are such that one of them exceeds the other by 9 and their sum is 81. What is the larger number?

    (a) 36   (b) 45
    (c) 48   (d) 56

29. In an army camp there were provision for 423 men for 36 days. If 324 men attended the camp, how long did the provision last?

    (a) 42 days   (b) 43 days
    (c) 47 days   (d) 48 days

30. A bus covers 225 km in 3 hours and a train covers 600 km in 5 hours. What is the ratio of their speeds?

(a) 3:5   (b) 5:7

(c) 5:8   (d) 3:8

31. 20 boys can dig a pitch in 12 hours. How long will 16 boys take to do it?

(a) 10 hours   (b) 15 hours

(c) 18 hours   (d) 20 hours

32. How many lines can be drawn passing through two given points

(a) One   (b) Two

(c) Three   (d) Unlimited

33. What is the maximum number of points of intersection of three lines in a plane?

(a) 1   (b) 2

(c) 3   (d) 0

34. The cost of fencing a rectangular field at Rs 24 per meter is Rs 1920. If its length is 27 m then what is its breadth?

(a) 12 m   (b) 13 m

(c) 15 m   (d) 16 m

35. How many square tiles each of side 0.5 m will be required to pave the floor of a room which is 4 m long and 3 m broad?

(a) 48   (b) 44

(c) 56   (d) 60

36. A brick is an example of a

(a) Cube   (b) Cuboid

(c) Cylinder   (d) Prism

37. The angles of a quadrilateral are 3:4:5:6. What is the difference of largest and smallest angle of quadrilateral?

(a) 20°   (b) 30°

(c) 40°   (d) 60°

38. In an isosceles Δ ABC, the bisectors of ∠B & ∠C meet at a point O. If ∠A = 40° then ∠BOC = ?

(a) 80°   (b) 90°

(c) 100°   (d) 110°

39. In the adjoining figure if ∠D + ∠E = 105°. What is the value of ∠F.

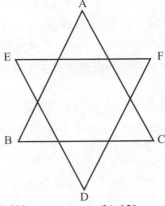

(a) 60°   (b) 65°

(c) 70°   (d) 75°

40. The ratio of length of a field to its width is 5:3. What is its length if the width is 42 m?

(a) 60 m   (b) 65 m

(c) 70 m   (d) 72 m

41. If $144 : x : : x : 121$ then what is the value of x ?

(a) 112   (b) 122

(c) 132   (d) 142

42. The cost of 5 banana is Rs. 25. There what is the cost of 5 dozen of banana?

(a) Rs. 200   (b) Rs. 240

(c) Rs. 280   (d) Rs. 300

43. What is the value of x if $\dfrac{x}{8} - \dfrac{1}{2} = \dfrac{x}{6} - 2$?

(a) 28   (b) 32

(c) 36   (d) 40

44. What is the value of P if $3(2 - 5P) - 2(1 - 6P) = 1$?

(a) 1   (b) $\dfrac{1}{2}$

(c) $\dfrac{1}{3}$ (d) 2

45. What must be subtracted from $a^2 - 3a + 5$ to obtain $5a^2 - 7a + 9$?

(a) $-3a^2 + 4a + 4$

(b) $-4a^2 + 4a - 4$

(c) $4a^2 - 4a + 4$

(d) None of these

46. By how much does 5 exceed $5x - 7y - 7$?

(a) $-5x + 7y + 12$ (b) $5x - 7y - 12$

(c) $5x - 7y$ (d) None of these

47. What is the co-efficient of a^2bc in $-6xba^2c$?

(a) -6 (b) $-6x$

(c) $-6bx$ (d) $-6abc$

48. Among 2.007, 2.067, 2.607 and 2.67 which is the largest?

(a) 2.607   (b) 2.67

(c) 2.007   (d) 2.067

49. $0.404 + 0.004 + 4.044 + 4.444 = ?$

(a) 8.896   (b) 8.886

(c) 8.096   (d) 8.806

50. The length of a rectangular hall is 5 m more than its breadth. If the perimeter is 74 m. What is the area of rectangle?

(a) $332m^2$ (b) $334m^2$

(c) $336m^2$ (d) $338m^2$

Answer Key

1. (c)	2. (b)	3. (a)	4. (c)	5. (b)	6. (b)	7. (c)	8. (c)	9. (d)	10 (b)
11. (b)	12. (b)	13. (c)	14. (b)	15. (d)	16. (c)	17. (a)	18. (c)	19. (b)	20. (a)
21. (b)	22. (a)	23. (d)	24. (b)	25. (c)	26. (d)	27. (d)	28. (b)	29. (c)	30. (c)
31. (b)	32. (a)	33. (a)	34. (b)	35. (a)	36. (b)	37. (d)	38. (d)	39. (d)	40. (c)
41. (c)	42. (d)	43. (c)	44. (a)	45. (b)	46. (a)	47. (b)	48. (b)	49. (a)	50. (c)